How Divorce Affects Offspring

How Divorce Affects Offspring

A Research Approach

Michael R. Stevenson

Ball State University

and

Kathryn N. Black

Purdue University—University of Arizona

WestviewPress

A Division of HarperCollins*Publishers*

Developmental Psychology Series
Wendell Jeffrey, Series Editor

Peer Prejudice and Discrimination,
Harold D. Fishbein

Communication Development During Infancy,
Lauren B. Adamson

Reading and Writing Acquisition: A Developmental Neuropsychological Perspective,
Virginia Wise Berninger

Children's Numbers, Catherine Sophian

How Divorce Affects Offspring: A Research Approach,
Michael R. Stevenson and Kathryn N. Black

Human Auditory Development, Lynne A. Werner and G. Cameron Marean

Published in 1996 in the United States of America by Westview Press, Inc., 5500 Central Avenue, Boulder, Colorado 80301-2877, and in the United Kingdom by Westview Press, 12 Hid's Copse Road, Cumnor Hill, Oxford OX2 9JJ

Library of Congress Cataloging-in-Publication Data
Stevenson, Michael R.
    How divorce affects offspring : a research approach / Michael R. Stevenson, Kathryn N. Black.
        p.   cm.
    Originally published: Madison, Wis. : Brown & Benchmark, 1995.
    Includes bibliographical references and index.
    ISBN 0-8133-3009-2 (pbk.)
    1. Children of divorced parents—Psychology.   2. Adult children of divorced parents—Psychology.   3. Divorce—Psychological aspects.
I. Black, Kathryn N.   II. Title.
HQ777.5.S74   1996
306.874—dc20   96-1279
                                                                                CIP

The paper used in this publication meets the requirements of the American National Standard for Permanence of Paper for Printed Library Materials Z39.48-1984.

10   9   8   7   6   5   4   3   2

CONTENTS

7   Romantic Relationships 85

8   Antisocial Behavior 100

9   Mental Health and Intervention 113

PREFACE

In our experience, there is bias and inconsistency in much of what is written about the effects of divorce on offspring. When interested students have asked for appropriate resources, we have been hard-pressed to respond without providing a long list of contradictory sources. Much of what is currently available reflects the cultural bias that parental divorce is one of the worst things that can happen to offspring.

This book has grown out of our desire to provide a comprehensive, accessible, balanced, and readable resource for upper-level undergraduate and graduate students who are interested in the effects of divorce upon offspring. We also hope that it will be useful to parents and practicing professionals who are not familiar with the empirical literature addressing this situation. Our primary goal is to evaluate and summarize the empirical literature in this field. However, we illustrate important points with examples drawn from autobiographies completed as part of a class assignment or from client histories based on one of the author's (KNB) counseling with families who are experiencing separation and divorce. We have selected life stories that describe problems in order to show possible results and that even difficult situations can have a positive resolution. Although the individuals involved may recognize themselves, there is insufficient information for anyone else to make an identification.

In an attempt to be consistent, we have made a variety of decisions about terminology that are consistent with our theoretical perspectives and our values. Given the variety of terms that have been used in the past, we will often use different terms from those that appeared in the original sources.

We use the term *sex* to refer to the male-female dichotomy that we believe to be originally based on anatomy. We prefer *gender roles* rather than *sex roles,* as these are socially constructed. We use the terms

African-American and *Caucasian* to refer to the most-often studied racial categories. We use *divorced* for those persons who were married and have not remarried; *married* and *remarried* are used as separate and mutually-exclusive categories. When it is not possible to be more specific, we use *single-parent* to refer to a heterogeneous group of mothers and fathers that may include the formerly married whether due to divorce, death, or never having been married. When the gender of the parent can be specified, we use *single mother* or *single father.* We avoid terms like *broken home* and *intact* families in favor of *divorced families* and *non-divorced families,* terms that are less value-laden and more specific.

Each chapter begins with a preview of the chapter's contents and ends with a summary of the main points. We attempt to be as specific in our generalizations as the data allow. Our first chapter provides a context for our review of research and discusses the prevalence of divorce. In chapter 2, we consider the way experts reach their conclusions and what we need to know about methodology in order to reach more accurate conclusions. Chapter 3 describes children's immediate reactions to the breakup of the family. A distinction has sometimes been made between short-term and long-term effects. However, there is no standard for differentiating between these categories, and studies frequently do not report the amount of time since the divorce. For this reason, we have focused on topics rather than on the questions of short-term versus long-term effects, and we make generalizations concerning the length of time since the divorce only when the data allow.

In the next six chapters, we consider different aspects of the lives and adjustment of offspring of divorce. Chapter 4 describes family relationships. Chapters 5 to 9 consider effects on cognitive development, gender-role development, and romantic relationships, as well as antisocial behavior, other problem behaviors, and possible interventions. These chapters are intentionally written so that they can be read in any order. We have followed the typical sequence used in introductory psychology and child psychology texts, however, and begin with cognitive variables followed by personality and social variables. Finally, in chapter 10, we address questions that are of concern to the larger culture, summarize what is known about the differences between offspring in divorced and non-divorced families, and make suggestions for social policy and future research.

Acknowledgments

Writing this text was a collaboration between two authors who have worked together in various capacities for over 15 years. It is difficult even for the authors to determine who was responsible for any particular passage or conclusion. As a result, the order of authorship was determined by the flip of a coin.

The authors acknowledge Deirdre Black LeMire, Amanda K. Black, and other offspring of divorce who provided the impetus for this book. We hope that our analysis of the literature will be a positive influence, either directly or indirectly, for families experiencing divorce. We wish to thank the many people who read drafts of the manuscript, including William E. Martin, Ph.D., and Shirley A. Stevenson. Thanks also to those who offered in-depth analyses at various draft stages, including Paul R. Amato, University of Nebraska–Lincoln; Mark A. Fine, University of Dayton; and John Santrock, University of Texas at Dallas. We especially wish to thank the students at Purdue University who read various drafts of the manuscript as it was being prepared and who provided, as part of their course work, many of the autobiographies that are included in the text. Support and encouragement came from many people, including Max E. Miller, Ph.D., and Linda Chapman.

The analyses and interpretations contained in this book are those of the authors and do not necessarily reflect the views of the authors' employers or affiliations.

Introduction

Preview

Divorce has had a dramatic impact on how we think about families and the lives of children. It seems fair to say that most people in our society believe that divorce has detrimental effects on the lives of offspring. In this introductory chapter, we explore the extent and possible consequences of such beliefs. We also discuss how often divorce occurs and the extent to which the experiences of offspring of divorce differ.

Perceptions and Stereotypes of the Effects of Divorce

Sue Grafton, a successful mystery writer, has said, "One of my theories is that no one with a happy childhood ever amounts to much in this world. They're so well-adjusted, they never are driven to achieve anything" (*USA Today,* 1992). Grafton's parents were both alcoholics and she had a troubled early life, which she interprets as having been good

1

for her in the long run. She said, "When you grow up in a dysfunctional household you quickly tune into what's going on under the surface. From age 5 or 6, I was scanning figuring out all the stuff not being discussed. . . ."

Like Ms. Grafton, people generally have a need to understand and explain their personal history. They also need to draw conclusions about the effects of real-life situations, including the aspects that appear harmful. Offspring of divorce are no different, and the life stories that we present in subsequent chapters help to illustrate this. All persons, not just scientists, continually process information and make predictions. Psychologists and social scientists do this with explicit theories, but everyone has implicit theories. It is likely that readers of this book already have some opinions regarding possible effects of divorce on children. Most people are convinced that there are effects, and that they are detrimental.

Preconceived beliefs about members of groups are referred to as stereotypes or schemas. Current stereotypes of the offspring of divorce present a rather negative image (Amato, 1991). For example, teachers expect a child of divorce to have more problems (Ball, Newman, & Scheuren, 1984). Because stereotypes can influence our expectations, it is not surprising that teachers' and school children's judgments of a child's academic, emotional, and social functioning were negatively influenced by the belief that the child's parents were divorced (Guttman, Geva, & Gefen, 1988).

These negative stereotypes may also lead to selective memory. After reading a varied description of a child, college students remembered more negative than positive traits if they had been told that the parents were divorced (Amato, 1991). Teachers who knew that children were from homes with divorced parents rated children more negatively than those who were not aware of the family marital structure (Santrock & Tracy, 1978). However, a similar 1986 study that used videotapes and asked observers to rate behaviors of children who were described as either from divorced or non-divorced homes did not find an effect (Goldstein-Henaday, Green, & Evans, 1986). Perhaps these biases about the effects of divorce only operate in situations with some ambiguity.

In addition to influencing our thoughts about others who may have experienced parental divorce, these cultural beliefs may also influence how offspring of divorce think of themselves. Our experiences with students and professionals have produced many examples. One young man who was thinking about becoming engaged asked, "Is it true that I'm more likely to get a divorce because my parents are divorced?" A high school student whose parents divorced 15 years earlier brought a psychology text which stated that girls living with their single mothers following divorce are likely to be inappropriately seductive toward males. She was wondering what this meant for her. An elementary school teacher had a student in her class who was not paying attention; she commented, "But his folks are going through a divorce, so I don't suppose there is anything that can be done about this, is there?" Although people seem convinced that there is some effect of divorce, they are unsure what it might be. Students taking a course on the effects of divorce upon offspring have commented, "My fiance came from a family of divorce and I want to understand him better and see what kinds of problems we are going to have," and "My parents had a messy divorce when I was little. I think it affected me badly and I want to find out how."

When one asks about the effects of parental divorce, responses commonly focus on negative outcomes. It would, of course, be surprising if a major life event did not have some effect. But we should remember that even unpleasant and undesired experiences may have some positive results. Weiss (1979) suggested some time ago that as a result of their changing role in the family, children who have experienced divorce may become more mature.

In fact, the vast majority of children of divorce will be able to offer examples of some positive outcomes (Black, 1982). Common ones include the cessation of parental fighting, learning to be behaviorally independent, and being more psychologically aware than peers. There may also be some outcomes that are not readily classified as either positive or negative. For example, divorce may lead offspring to focus on their parents as individuals rather than as a joint entity.

In addition to the belief that all outcomes of divorce are negative, another common idea that should be challenged is that parental divorce will create stress only for children who are living at home. The small amount of literature concerning college-age offspring of divorce suggests that this event is as distressing for them as for younger children. A recent book (Fintushel & Hillard, 1991) describes the reactions of 100 adult offspring whose parents divorced when they were between 18 and 46 years of age. The authors conclude that these divorces were characterized by bitter disturbances and that much harm is done in the initial phase of such divorces because parents are unprepared for the intensity of their adult children's reactions.

What difference does it make what one believes about the effects of divorce? Certain beliefs may affect one's subsequent actions. For example, couples may decide not to divorce, "for the sake of the children."

Furthermore, divorcing adults may find that others make negative judgments about what they have done. Consider this scenario: a couple with little in common marry when still in high school because she is pregnant. After a second child and six years of marriage, the wife eventually continues her education and then chooses to divorce. Relatives tell her that she is harming her children and that if she were a responsible mother, she would not do this. As a result, stress for this single mother is increased by disapproval from those she cares about.

The offsprings' beliefs may also affect their own reactions to their parents' divorce. For example, an 8-year-old boy seeing a school counselor says that from what his parents have told him, divorce doesn't sound so bad, as he will continue to see both of them. However, he is afraid that when his friends find out, they won't want to play with him anymore. Richard Gardner (1970), a well-known psychiatrist and author of books about dealing with divorce, suggested that children from non-divorced families may be hostile or demeaning to those whose parents divorce, and that this negative reaction arises from the prejudice of their parents. Fortunately, the stigma associated with divorce has decreased over the last two decades (Brandwein, Brown, & Fox, 1974; Thornton, 1985), although it has not disappeared. Certainly both children and parents now have less reason to see themselves as different when divorce occurs.

Although a person may hold some beliefs about the effects of divorce, these beliefs are probably based upon experience, or on observations of a particularly dramatic situation. It is perhaps inevitable for individuals to make generalizations based upon available information. But this process may not produce an accurate depiction of what typically happens when parents divorce.

Unfortunately, published generalizations made by people thought to be experts may also be biased due to limited data. For example, Judith Wallerstein disseminated her findings in books (e.g., Wallerstein & Kelly, 1980; Wallerstein & Blakeslee, 1989) and in magazines, including *Redbook* and the *New York Times Magazine*. These reports have promulgated her view, also elaborated in professional journals (e.g., Wallerstein, 1991), that divorce will leave a "universal legacy" of anxiety. Similarly, *Reader's Digest,* which claims to be the "world's most widely read magazine" and which sells over 28 million copies monthly in 16 languages, published an article on parental divorce (Whitehead, 1993). The author argued that the effects of divorce are profound, claiming that parental divorce is associated with decreases in well-being and in school performance, and increases in teen suicide and juvenile crime. She concluded that as a result of the prevalence of divorce, "This may be the first generation to do worse psychologically and socially than its parents" (p. 123). Although these conclusions alone are disturbing, more significant is that much of the information reaching large audiences supports the biased view that there are major and long-term detrimental effects for most children of divorce.

The Prevalence of Divorce

Approximately 95 percent of the adults in the United States marry at some time in their lives, and about 95 percent of these marriages create a family with children. Since colonial days, some marriages have ended in divorce (Riley, 1991), although in the recent past, marital disruption by divorce was a relatively rare phenomenon. Society apparently considered divorce so undesirable that it was only allowed when a marital partner had exhibited some grievous fault such as alcoholism or infidelity. Divorce has been considered particularly undesirable when children were involved.

Around 1970, the divorce rate began increasing dramatically: nearly 30 percent of the couples who were married in 1952 were divorced by their twenty-fifth wedding anniversary; couples married in 1967 took only ten years to experience similar attrition. Although the overall rate of divorce peaked by 1980 and has leveled off since then, in 1990 there were 2.4 million marriages and 1.2 million divorces in the United States (Ahlburg & DeVita, 1992). The divorce rate in the United States remains among the highest in the world, but it varies with such sociological factors as age at marriage, state of residence, religion, and education, as well as psychological variables such as alcoholism, abuse, the presence of handicapped children, unemployment, and other family stress factors.

Another change associated with the increase in divorce is "no-fault" divorce; that is, divorce no longer requiring one partner to demonstrate that the other has done something socially unacceptable. Legally this is referred to as the "irretrievable breakdown of the marriage." In addition to changing the laws concerning the basis for ending a marriage, some states have also changed the terminology. For example, in Indiana a marriage does not legally end in "divorce" but in "dissolution." However, because of the general use of the term, we will continue to use "divorce" throughout this book.

When divorce involves children under 18, state laws also govern some aspects of what happens to the children. This includes legal custody, where children reside, when they visit a noncustodial parent, and financial support. Census data for 1991 indicated that nearly one in eight families was headed by a single parent. This is double the proportion in 1970 (Ahlburg & DeVita, 1992). In 1991, there were 4.5 million divorced mothers with children living with them following divorce and an additional 1.9 million separated mothers with children. There were also over 1 million divorced fathers with children living with them and an additional 373,000 separated fathers with children (U.S. Bureau of Census, 1992). Ahlburg and DeVita (1992) also report that single-parent families represented one in five Caucasian families with children, one in three Hispanic families with children, and six in ten African-American families with children.

In the 1980s and 1990s, about 35 percent of all minor children will experience parental divorce, occurring for varied reasons. Sometimes the divorces are amicable, and sometimes they involve great conflict, including physical violence. Custody is determined by the courts in about 10 percent of cases, whereas agreements are reached by the divorcing couple or through professional mediation in about 90 percent of divorces. Following divorce, between 85 percent and 90 percent of children will be in the custody of their mothers.

Although still a small proportion, the incidence of single-father families since 1970 has increased at a faster rate than that of single-mother families. Between 1970 and 1980, there was a 40 percent increase in the number of single-father families. From 1980 to 1990, the number increased by an additional 66 percent (U.S. Bureau of Census, 1992). Often children reside with their fathers as the result of an informal arrangement, rather than because of a legal decree. There are a few children, probably less than 1 percent, who live with someone other than a parent after parental divorce; this is most often grandparents.

The majority of divorced parents eventually remarry. Apparently, most people feel that it is not marriage that is at fault but that a particular marriage did not work. Remarriage occurs most often within two to five years, but there are some who are already engaged by the time they go to court for the dissolution, and there are others who will never remarry. Generally speaking, about three fourths of men and about two thirds of women remarry. These numbers differ because men are more likely to remarry someone younger who has not previously been married. To complicate things further, about one in ten couples who have divorced remarry one another (Furstenberg & Spanier, 1984). Following a remarriage, children are sometimes born to the new marriage. In 1985, over 2 million families were living with both stepchildren and biological children of that couple.

Remarriages are also subject to divorce. The divorce rate for second marriages depends, in part, upon whether there are minor children from previous marriages. The divorce rate is about the same as for first marriages when there are no children, but more remarriages end in divorce when both spouses have minor children from previous marriages (Martin & Bumpass, 1989), and fewer remarriages end in divorce when women give birth in the second marriage (Wineberg, 1992).

Some offspring of divorce face more unusual circumstances. A study by Finkelhor, Hotaling, and Sedlak (1992), of a large sample of randomly selected households suggests that approximately 5 percent to 8 percent of children whose parents have been divorced have been abducted by a family member. In 1988 more than 350,000 children were abducted, mostly by fathers involved in disputes over child custody that occurred at the time of the first separation or even years later. These episodes typically lasted two days to a week, although 10 percent lasted a month or more. Only about half of these abductions were reported to the police, perhaps because the children were not really missing but rather were not where they were supposed to be. Hegar and Greif (1991; Greif & Hegar, 1993) surveyed families who sought help from missing children's organizations. Generally, the abductions involved only one child, who was most often under seven years of age. Both mothers and fathers were abductors. Although children reacted in a variety of ways, those who were abused, were missing for long periods, or who witnessed violence were more likely to have difficulty adapting.

Each year, unknown numbers of children are taken into hiding by one parent who believes that the child is being sexually abused by the other parent. Society's League Against Molestation is a group that helps mothers and children go into hiding rather than carry out a court order for unsupervised visitation with the suspected abuser. According to a study by the American Bar Association (*USA Today,* 1989), sexual abuse is charged in 2 percent to 10 percent of disputed visitation cases. This constitutes between 1,800 and 9,000 cases yearly. Thoennes and Tjaden (1990) also concluded that only a small proportion of contested custody and visitation cases involved sexual abuse allegations. They reviewed cases from a variety of courts in the United States and found that in at least one third and possibly as much as one half of these instances, abuse had not, in fact, occurred.

In rare instances following estrangement, one marital partner attacks, injures, and/or kills the partner who left. Even more rarely, a parent attempts to injure a child. In May, 1991, a father from Indianapolis set fire to a car containing his children after receiving a summons for being delinquent in child support payments.

The Effects of Divorce on Offspring

The experiences of children whose parents divorce vary widely, and children may react in different ways to the same experience. Considering all of the possible permutations in the divorce process, we might ask how anyone could expect to make generalizations about the effects of divorce upon the offspring. Although it is not now possible to make broad generalizations, and it probably never will be, this doesn't mean that generalization is impossible. For example, we expect reactions to vary with characteristics of family functioning, offspring, and perhaps post-divorce family structure.

In contrast to others, this book is based on our evaluation and presentation of empirical research. It is clear that in a variety of disciplines for a variety of behaviors, the offspring of divorce have been found to be different "on the average" from those from non-divorced families. The major issue is whether it is accurate to say that these differences are "effects of divorce." Our goal is that as a result of reading this book, you will be more accurate and therefore probably more cautious in your generalizations and interpretations of research on the effects of divorce. Toward that end, we next turn our attention to methodological issues relevant to empirical research on offspring of divorce and discuss how "experts" reach conclusions concerning the effects of divorce on offspring.

Summary

- Current stereotypes suggest that divorce has harmful effects on offspring.
- These beliefs can have negative consequences for those who experience parental divorce and can influence the way that we perceive divorcing families.
- Most adults marry, although currently about one third of marriages end in divorce.
- Over a third of all minor children experience parental divorce. Many of these children will experience their parents' remarriages, as well.
- Although we are unable to predict how an individual will react to parental divorce, research does provide answers to some specific questions about the effects of divorce on offspring.

How Experts Reach
Their Conclusions

Preview

As noted in the previous chapter, our beliefs regarding the effects of divorce may be shaped by what we are told by experts, often as disseminated by the popular literature. However, expert opinion changes over time, and conclusions drawn by experts are often inconsistent. In this chapter, we describe how research on offspring is designed. We further consider how experts reach their conclusions and why this may result in disagreement.

Research Methodology

Researchers make distinctions between qualitative and quantitative methods. Although quantitative research has been favored over the past several decades, both types of research can contribute to our understanding, as well as our misunderstanding, of the effects of divorce.

Qualitative Data

Qualitative methods produce detailed reports of a few individuals and are useful for generating hypotheses. They can contribute to our understanding of offspring of divorce by describing in detail how people react to the life experiences associated with parental divorce. (The life stories that appear in subsequent chapters serve the same purpose.) However, qualitative data should not be used as a basis for broad generalizations.

Case Studies and In-Depth Interviews

Much pioneering research in psychology has consisted of case studies that were in-depth analyses of a few individuals. The well-known works of Freud and Piaget are obvious examples. Light and Pillemer (1984) argued that case studies are crucial in the early stages of science when scripts are being formed. Scripts, our expectations about recurring events, are important in influencing the belief system and professional behavior of scientists, as well as of people in general.

In the early days of making systematic observations and presenting them in writing, researchers in the field of divorce also made use of case studies. They learned a great deal about a particular person, either an adult or a child, who had experienced divorce. Information from case studies and other qualitative data led to scripts that helped to manage information. Most frequently, the subjects of these studies were clients in therapy whose behavior was interpreted within a psychiatric or psychoanalytic framework.

In general, psychoanalytic theory, the early prototypic theory of personality development, predicts that a father's absence, as in the case of divorce, leads to unclear or confused gender identification, with possible resultant homosexuality or difficulties in heterosexual relationships when children who have this experience reach young adulthood. The theory also suggests that absence during particular periods of the child's development will have different, although always detrimental, effects (Freud, 1949, 1950; Leonard, 1966; Neubauer, 1960).

Although many case studies supported these conclusions (e.g., McDermott, 1968; Trunnell, 1968; Westman, 1972), Plant (1944) more cautiously concluded that "there isn't one 'symptom,' any one pattern, that belongs to them" (p. 812). More recently, Lamers (1977) suggested that the detrimental effects that are found need not be permanent if the appropriate care is offered. Nonetheless, taken together, psychoanalytic theory and selected case studies appear to have been important in the development of an influential script concerning the detrimental effects of divorce.

Those with some sophistication in the scientific method will not be surprised to learn that case studies are not appropriate as a basis for broad generalizations regarding the effects of divorce (Plant, 1944; Ferri, 1976; Luepnitz, 1978; Berlinsky & Biller, 1982). It is likely that these individuals represent only those who were the most adversely affected. We could expect to find dramatic differences between people who come for therapy and those who do not. The obvious criticism concerns the likely atypical nature of clients in therapy. It is also true, however, that any one instance is not likely to represent an entire sample. Although inappropriate as a basis for broad generalizations, consideration of a number of case studies may be useful as a source of insight into the potential consequences of divorce. Qualitative information of this type can be particularly useful when conflicts arise in literature or when it seems desirable to bring about a change in our scripts (Light & Pillemer, 1984).

As mentioned in chapter 1, an ongoing study (Wallerstein & Kelly, 1980; Wallerstein & Blakeslee, 1989) continues to shape our expectations about the effects of divorce. The California Children of Divorce Study was begun in the early 1970s with 60 divorcing families and involved 131 children aged 3 to 18 from Marin County. Available children were first interviewed close to the decisive separation and then at post-divorce intervals of 18 months, 5 years, 10 years, and 15 years. The children in the initial sample were not retarded and had not been in psychological treatment prior to the separation. The parents were Caucasian, well-educated, literate, and without pathology.

Reports of this study include descriptions of both parent-child behaviors and of the offspring's general adjustment. The data were gathered using unstructured, in-depth interviews of unknown reliability. The interview protocol was not standardized, although each participant was asked similar questions.

Although this study provides some insight into the dynamics of divorcing families, it does not provide adequate data for broad generalizations about the effects of divorce. The sample was not representative of divorcing families, and no data were gathered from non-divorcing families. Although the parents were selected to have no pathology, Wallerstein reported that one-quarter of the families had experienced violence in the marriage. Further, 10 years after the separation, half of the women and almost a third of the men were still intensely angry at their former spouse. Wallerstein judged that at 10 years post-divorce, one quarter of the mothers and one fifth of the fathers had such emotional or behavioral problems that they were unable to meet the challenge of being a parent.

As is common with the clinical interview method, information gathered from individuals was examined for patterns common to others. Statistical analysis of such data is limited, with results typically reported as percentages or proportions. For example, Wallerstein reports that there was moderate to severe depression in over one third of the original sample 5 years after the separation; a significant number of young men and women at the 10-year mark appeared to her to be troubled, drifting, and underachieving; yet over half of the children in the study were judged as compassionate and competent people.

Findings like these are difficult to interpret. Wallerstein is clearly convinced that divorce has significantly and often negatively affected the lives of these people. However, it is unclear how her convictions influenced the interview process and her conclusions. Furthermore, this design does not allow us to determine whether, without divorce, fewer of these young adults would have been drifting and troubled, or how many people from non-divorced families are compassionate and competent. Without data from a similar group of Caucasian and middle class California residents who have not experienced parental divorce, we have no way of knowing whether to attribute problems to the divorce, to some other family characteristic or dysfunctional behavior, or to the way in which the interviews were conducted.

Qualitative research produces data that are rich in detail. However, these data can be easily misinterpreted when not approached with appropriate caution. The next approach to consider sacrifices some detail, but often makes use of the group-comparisons method absent in qualitative research.

Quantitative Data

In contrast to qualitative methods, researchers using quantitative methods attempt to assess the behavior of large numbers of people by counting behaviors or by using measures that produce numerical scores. These numbers can be manipulated using statistical tests, the results of which can be used to support generalizations about offspring of divorce.

Group Comparisons

Considerable research has made use of the "father-absence paradigm," which compares groups of father-absent and father-present offspring. These studies investigate links between family structure and various outcomes in offspring. Typically, the offspring complete questionnaires, or their behavior is rated by others. Raters have included parents, teachers, or specially trained observers. The results are usually evaluated statistically by the comparison of means using an analysis of variance.

The father-absence paradigm is useful in describing how children who experience the breakup of their parents' marriage differ in general from those who have not experienced parental divorce. However, given the quasi-experimental nature of the design (Campbell & Stanley, 1963), it is not helpful in determining why these differences occur. Comparison of groups will result in accurate information about divorce as a cause only if we randomly select a large sample of two-parent families and bring about divorce in one half of the families, something that is obviously neither ethical nor feasible.

Early research utilizing this paradigm usually compared convenient groups of children who happened to fit particular definitions of "father-absent" and "father-present." Such a conceptualization may at first seem straightforward. However, it is an oversimplification of a complex situation. For example, fathers can be "absent" for a variety of reasons, and the father-absent groups often included some children with deceased fathers. Considerable research suggests that we should not make broad generalizations based on data from mixed groups of father-absent children (Herzog & Sudia, 1973; Shinn, 1978; Stevenson & Black, 1988). Unfortunately, results of these father-absence studies have been used as a basis for generalizations concerning divorce (Rosenfeld & Rosenstein, 1973).

Another problem with this design is that "absent" but living fathers also differ in the amount of contact they have with their families. Earl and Lohmann (1978) showed that 51 percent of their "father-absent" boys saw their father regularly and that all of the boys had access to some adult male who could serve as a role model. Forgatch, Patterson and Skinner (1988) reported that less than 10 percent of their sample had no contact with their fathers. On the other hand, in "father-present" homes, the father can be perceived by his offspring as unloving and unaccepting (Fleck, Fuller, Malin, Miller, & Acheson, 1980). This condition has been described as "father psychological absence" and may represent a parent-child relationship similar to that associated with divorce.

To complicate things further, what is the correct group assignment when a remarriage occurs? What about those instances of multiple divorce or remarriage? Even if one were to make certain that the extent of the father's absence were the same, the cause of divorce was breakdown in a marital relationship. This is likely to mean that the children made different observations of parental interaction as well as interpretations of what marriages are like. Put simply, the terms "father absent" and "father present" appear to be inappropriate for describing these groups.

In addition to these methodological problems, this paradigm is based on the implicit assumption that the "traditional family," one with an employed father and a homemaker mother, is the ideal setting in which to rear children. In spite of the fact that these families account for only 11 percent of families (Scarr, 1984), it is considered the norm against which other "lesser" families are compared. With the father-absence paradigm, the behavior of offspring from two-parent homes is taken as the norm. When differences occur, single-parent children are generally considered deviant, regardless of whether their scores are lower or higher than those in never-divorced groups, and without consideration of whether the behavior of either group falls within what is considered normal or healthy. In one study (Jacobson & Ryder, 1969), adult married couples where one member had a deceased parent felt closer to one another than couples from two-parent families. Rather than viewing increased marital closeness as a possible positive outcome, these data were used to support an argument that these couples were overly dependent upon one another.

The implicit assumption of traditional family superiority is inherent in some terminology. Writers may refer to "father absence" and "broken homes" in contrast to "intact families." To avoid this assumption, others describe family structure more accurately as "single-mother" families, or as "two-parent homes." This assumption that the traditional family is superior is often demonstrated when these studies are used as the basis for inferences about the influence of fathers on child development. Such studies usually imply that "father absence" will be detrimental and that any differences between the groups are attributable to the positive influence of the present father.

A well-known study by Hetherington (1972) is a good example of research using the father-absence paradigm. Hetherington interviewed and observed three groups of 12 lower- and lower middle- class, first-born, adolescent Caucasian girls at a community recreation center. The first group had both mothers and fathers living at home. The second group included girls whose parents had divorced and who had minimal contact with their fathers. The third group included girls whose fathers had died. None of the girls had male siblings. In the "father-absent" households, no males had been living in the home since separation from the father had occurred, and none of the girls interacted regularly with any other significant males. There were no differences between the groups in mean age or education of the participants, in occupation, education, or age of the parents, in maternal employment, in religious affiliation, or in number of siblings. Such careful participant selection controls a number of variables that may mediate the relation between family structure and child outcomes.

The results suggested that both daughters of divorced mothers and daughters of widows felt insecure around male peers and male adults. However, this insecurity was displayed behaviorally in very different ways. Daughters of divorced mothers spent extensive time at the boys' end of the recreation center and displayed attention-seeking behavior with the male interviewer. Daughters of widows generally refused to interact with boys and avoided interaction with the adult male interviewer. Ratings of daughters from two-parent homes fell in between.

In a description reported in *Psychology Today,* Hetherington (1973) went so far as to describe daughters of divorcees as "promiscuous" and "clumsily erotic with men." She also suggested that, "Girls whose fathers had died exhibited severe sexual anxiety, shyness and discomfort around males" (p. 49).

This study is often cited in child psychology textbooks. After reading about these findings, a female student whose parents had divorced publicly exclaimed, "For all these years I've had a great excuse for being promiscuous, and I haven't been taking advantage of it!"

Significantly, other studies using this same general design and procedure have been unable to replicate these findings. For now, it is important to consider why this one study is so widely cited while others that do not support it are not mentioned. Is it because this was the first study and the findings were so dramatic? Perhaps it is because such findings match our stereotypes concerning negative outcomes.

Because subsequent studies produced different results, data from the Hetherington study must be interpreted carefully. As noted above, Hetherington very carefully chose a sample that did not have continuing interactions with males. Perhaps this or other controls mean that her findings apply only to a small portion of daughters whose parents divorce. However, it is also possible that this is one of those "by chance" erroneous findings, which occur even with well-designed studies. Given the typical level of statistical significance, if no difference exists between two populations, about 1 in 20 studies will erroneously conclude that the groups differ.

As father-absence research became more sophisticated, researchers began to take into consideration that variables other than the cause of the absence might be associated with father absence, and that these variables could actually be the ones affecting the outcome measures. For example, as we discussed in chapter 1, the incidence of divorce differs by social class. One way to control for social class is to study only a narrowly defined group, the middle class or the working class. Social class is ordinarily defined by education, occupation, or income. In a divorced family, though, do you use ratings of the mother's social class, the father's social class, or some combination? Do you use information prior to the separation/divorce or following it? Various reports conclude that there is a decline in the standard of living for women and their children after the divorce. Peterson (1989) used data from the National Longitudinal Surveys of Mature Women for the years 1967 and 1977 and found that several years after divorce, the standard of living was reduced by from 5 to 20 percent. Duncan and Hoffman (1985) also reported a decrease in financial well-being after marital dissolution. The most dramatic finding was that of Weitzman (1985) who reported that a sample of California women experienced a 73 percent standard of living decline in the first year after divorce. It seems likely that there would be a significant difference in expendable income between one- and two-parent families, even if they were from the same social class.

As we have shown, "father-absent" and "father-present" groups differ in many ways. When groups of children from divorced and non-divorced families are compared, there will be problems matching groups, as there are "too many potentially important extraneous variables" (Blechman, 1982; p. 182). As Pederson (1976) concluded some years ago, this paradigm has outlived its usefulness and should be replaced with the study of more specific components of family experience.

Process-Oriented Research

The father-absence paradigm produced results showing that, on the average, offspring from divorced families differ from those of other families. The group comparison design implies that the cause of these differences is the structure of the family. However, we know that the divorce decree itself did not bring about the effects, and that the effects were at the least mediated by some other things. Concern for mediating variables such as social class and family size has had a long history, with Henry Biller describing them since his early reviews of the literature (e.g., 1974). Recently, professionals have emphasized the importance of the quality of the marital relationship, the amount of conflict in the home, and the quality of the parent-child relationship (e.g., Amato, 1987; Barber & Eccles, 1992; Dornbusch, Carlsmith, Bushwall, Ritter, Leiderman, Hastorf & Gross, 1985; Emery, 1982).

Terminology changes as approaches do, and we now find these qualities referred to as "process variables." To make significant advances in our knowledge, we must shift from attributing group differences to family structure and instead emphasize process variables (Emery, Hetherington, & Di Lalla, 1984). This means that in addition to child response measures, information is now gathered—either from the child, the parents, or by observers—about the entire family. One characteristic of process approaches is that more data are available for analysis.

This approach developed both because of changes in how professionals think about the problem and because of the availability of new statistical techniques for handling large amounts of data. Such complicated techniques as multiple regression analysis and path analysis have become practical only because of the development of computers.

Two examples of process-oriented research demonstrate that this approach yields information not available from group comparisons. In the first, Pederson, Rubenstein, and Yarrow (1979) studied infant functioning with samples of divorced fathers and non-divorced fathers. Although infants from these groups did differ, a measure of the amount of father interaction was a better predictor of the child's behavior than the divorced status.

Process-oriented research not only allows us to identify possible specific factors that differ between children in one- and two-parent families but also to determine which variables influence other variables. Such an approach, using structural modeling, is exemplified by a study by Forgatch, Patterson, and Skinner (1988). A number of investigators have found that boys from families of divorce are more likely to engage in antisocial behaviors. Forgatch et al. found that for many mothers, divorce produces high levels of stress, that such stress leads to inept discipline practices, and that it is these practices, rather than the divorce, per se, that lead to sons' antisocial behavior.

It should be apparent by now that there are a variety of ways to explore the effects of divorce on offspring, and that each of these general methods of research has its advantages and disadvantages. Some research questions require the rich detail provided by the case studies and clinical interviews. Other questions require more statistical sophistication and experimental control. Each approach makes its own unique contribution to our understanding of parental divorce. Relying heavily on one form of research while neglecting others is like constructing a puzzle without all of the pieces.

Research Choices

No matter what general approach is chosen, researchers must make other major decisions. These include deciding which hypotheses to test, which variables to measure, and which samples to study.

Choosing Variables

No one research project can attempt to answer every question regarding the effects of divorce on offspring. How do researchers decide what questions to ask and which variables to measure?

As we have suggested, most researchers have looked for harmful or negative effects, rarely considering possible positive outcomes (Barber & Eccles, 1992). More specifically, Scarr (1985) argued that our theories help to determine our findings. Theory guides inquiry through the questions raised, the framework of inquiry, and the interpretation of the results. Scientists, like all humans, tend to focus on data that will assimilate into their world view. Each of us is biased by the human tendency to seek information that is congruent with our beliefs. Scarr contends that due in part to the impact of the women's movement, our theories concerning so-called father-absent and "broken homes" are being reconstructed to focus on "alternative family" forms and "non-traditional families." Another factor in this changing emphasis is that it may be difficult for our or any society to maintain strong beliefs about the damaging effect of such a prevalent experience. These new orientations have led to different interpretations of the "facts" as well as to some new questions. On the basis of the life stories obtained from a case study protocol, we found that most children of divorce will report that there were positive effects, with some giving more positive than negative ones.

Both theory and past findings tend to influence the kind of variables that a researcher will choose. Much of the early work on the effects of father absence concerned the role of modeling and identification and was related to the belief that males needed a present father with whom to identify or relate. This absence was hypothesized to affect a wide variety of behaviors, including gender-role development and cognitive development. However, findings do not strongly support this assumption, even though many continue to make it when considering issues such as whether children do better in the custody of a parent of the same sex rather than that of the other sex.

Longitudinal versus Cross-Sectional Designs

For theoretical reasons, it seems likely that most children of divorce will be distressed at the time of separation and divorce because of the general loss and adaptation required. If this is the only variable involved, we might not expect effects to persist over time, except as additional adjustments to change are involved. Some researchers make a distinction between short-term and long-term effects in an attempt to differentiate between immediate reactions and those that persist over time or appear later. Clearly one important variable to be considered is the time since separation. However, this is not always simple to determine, because divorces are preceded by a series of separations and reconciliations. As a result, this variable is often excluded from statistical analyses.

The importance of the time since the divorce is related to whether the researcher gathers data from different cross-sectional samples, each seen at one period post-divorce, or whether the research will be longitudinal, following the same group of people over time. Longitudinal research is time-consuming and expensive, although it has some advantages.

For example, Wallerstein's (1991) use of a longitudinal design produced evidence for what she calls a "sleeper effect." This refers to an effect that is related to an earlier event, but which does not show up at first. As an example, Wallerstein reported that some females adapted well emotionally and socially to the original divorce when they were still at home, but that later they had difficulties in dealing with issues arising from trust in males and the development of a committed relationship. Other longitudinal studies, originated primarily for purposes other than for measuring the effects of divorce, examined that subsample of participants whose parents divorced while the study was being conducted. They provide fascinating information concerning the characteristics of children prior to divorce.

Block, Block, and Gjerde (1986) repeatedly assessed personality characteristics of a sample of California children over an 11-year period. Those children whose parents divorced at some time during the study were compared with children whose parents remained married. Even prior to their experience of divorce, the sons of divorced families exhibited behavior that was characterized by impulsiveness, aggression, and abundant but misguided energy. A finding of greater aggression in boys following divorce has been repeatedly noted in the literature. This study suggests that the divorce was not the cause, although it is likely that these behaviors grew from distressed family or marital interactions.

Cherlin et al. (1991) used national, longitudinal surveys from Great Britain and the United States to investigate the effects of divorce on children. All parents were together at the initial collection of data when the children were age 7 for the British study, and 7 to 11 for the U.S. study. A second set of data was gathered about four years later. Data from both countries indicate that much of what is usually considered the effect of divorce on children is visible before the parents separate.

For boys, the apparent effect of divorce on behavior problems and school achievement falls to levels that are not significantly different from zero once the variables of pre-existing behavior problems, achievement test scores, and family difficulties evident before the separation are taken into account statistically. For girls, including these pre-existing conditions also reduces but does not completely eliminate the effects of divorce.

These findings may be specific to the behaviors considered, or there might be an effect that will appear later; nevertheless, they suggest that many of the effects that we attribute to divorce may actually be the result of other things and would have occurred regardless of the divorce.

Selection of Measures

The selection of measures is dictated not only by the effect in which we are interested, but also by what measures are available and possible. It would seem relatively clear-cut to ask about things like intelligence test scores and grade point if we are interested in intellectual development. There are still practical considerations: will already-available group tests scores, which might allow a consideration of thousands of cases, be used, or should one administer more accurate individual tests to a much smaller sample? In the area of emotions and adjustments there are even more complicated decisions to make. Even when relatively objective ratings scales are used, it may be necessary to create measures of the chosen variable; then issues of the reliability or validity of the measures arise. In some cases (e.g., Hetherington, 1972), specific observational measures must be developed.

We must also ask whether children are the best judges of their own adjustment. Shortly after separation, adolescents in the California Children of Divorce study appeared to be adjusting better than children of other ages. However, they later gave an entirely different view, stating that they just could not acknowledge the extent to which they were upset. They could not tell others nor admit it even to themselves. Would others who lived with them be any better at making this judgment?

Studies now commonly make use of multiple measures, including ratings by the offspring themselves, their parents, or their teachers. Rather than combining all of these measures into one, it may be more desirable to use these in separate analyses. Achenbach, McConaughy, and Howell (1987) examined available research concerning the relationships between child self-report, parent report, and reports of others such as teachers or mental health workers. They concluded that there were modest relationships among these measures, and that each should be considered as one possible aspect of assessment. Amato and Keith (1991a) concluded that effects based on reports by parents and teachers were weaker than effects based on other sources.

There are a number of possible reasons for measures to differ. One is that the children are observed by others in different settings. Another is that each evaluator may have some possible bias. We have already noted that some teachers will be influenced by their knowledge of the family structure. Reactions may also be different at school or home. Some children have reported (Black, 1982) that they dealt with their reactions by concentrating on school, although they were upset when at home. Parents, as most observers, probably do best when reporting explicit behaviors and not children's distress. This might arise either because parents are in such distress themselves that they do not have the ability to see what is happening with their children or because some children tend to protect their parents and the parental relationship by not letting the parent know about the distress or anger.

Choice of Sample

There are two major kinds of questions that can be answered by empirical research. We may wish to describe the characteristics of a particular population. For example, we may want to know the frequency with which children become depressed following parental divorce. This question can be made more complicated by asking if there are differences between the sexes or for children of different ages. Alternatively, we may wish to make inferences about relationships between variables. For example, we might ask if the adjustment of offspring after divorce is affected by the nature of the relationship between the parents.

Research concerned with description requires certain kinds of samples from a population: random, representative, or stratified. To construct such a sample, we must first be able to identify the population to which we wish to generalize. One example might be all children in the United States whose parents divorced during 1993. In this case, a random and representative sample would be one where each child whose parents divorced during 1993, regardless of age, race, or any other characteristic, had an equal chance of being included in the study. In stratified samples, participants are chosen at random but based on particular characteristics. For example, a researcher interested in race differences can choose to stratify the sample on race so that approximately equal numbers of African-American children, Caucasian children, and Hispanic-American children are chosen for the study, even though such a sample would include different proportions of children in each category than what actually occurs in the population. Studies that do not use these kinds of samples should not be used to make descriptive generalizations.

Assuming that major relationships hold true for a variety of sub-populations, it is less important that samples used for generalizations about relationships be random or representative. In fact, researchers may choose samples to fit carefully constructed categories. As mentioned earlier, Hetherington (1972) chose the daughters of divorcées and daughters of widows in her study very carefully to control for the influence of a variety of variables.

Similarly, some have chosen to examine samples because they become available in unusual settings, such as mental health clinics, referrals to therapists, or juvenile detention centers. Although there are clear differences between atypical groups (Amato & Keith, 1991b, Stevenson & Black, 1988, Kanoy & Cunningham, 1984), such studies are useful in certain contexts. For example, Phares and Compas (1992) used data from clinical samples to determine that the risk for children associated with paternal psychopathology is comparable to that which is associated with maternal psychopathology.

The research by Wallerstein does not meet the criteria of representative sampling, and thus cannot validly be used to conclude anything about the frequency of pathology in the population of children of divorce. On the other hand, Wallerstein's data are useful in further demonstrating that there is a relationship between high parent conflict and a negative outcome for offspring.

We are not suggesting that only large-scale representative samples be studied. We may want to know specifically about subgroups such as therapy clients, or about ethnic or racial minorities. Further, studies using samples that are conveniently available may serve as a source of new hypotheses, or to confirm suggestions already in the literature.

Generalizations about the Effects of Divorce

It should be clear by now that the question, "Are there effects upon off-spring of parental divorce?" cannot be answered in a simple fashion. Generalizations will most likely refer to a particular sex at a particular developmental level for some specific point in the divorce process. Appropriate generalizations might take this form: preschool-aged males are more likely to be aggressive soon after parental separation than those who have not experienced divorce.

We have seen that studies are more likely to yield accurate statements about relationships than to accurately describe, as a group, the children of divorce. However, no matter which generalization is being sought, findings are likely to be specific to particular behaviors, and this relationship may be complicated. For example, Billingsham, Pillion, and Sauer (1991) found that adult women whose parents had divorced were both nonpermissive in their sexual attitudes and more permissive in their behavior as compared to adult women in non-divorced families. That is, they did not approve of the things that they nonetheless were doing.

Another example of the complexity of the field is that although we may find effects, the specific effects may be dramatically different. Hetherington (1989) has reported research involving the evaluation and behavior classification of children in late elementary school. Children 4 to 6 years post-divorce, compared to those with no family divorce, were more likely to be both in a group described as aggressive, impulsive, and insecure, as well as in one described as unusually caring, competent, and popular. The post-divorce males were more likely to be in the former and females in the latter grouping.

Why Do the Experts Disagree?

The purpose of doing research is to be able to make generalizations. Either because of the sample used or because of measurement errors, however, the generalizations from a particular study may be in error. One type of error occurs when the investigator concludes that there is not an effect when in fact one does exist in the underlying population. Another type of error is the reverse: the investigator concludes that there is an effect when in fact one does not exist in the underlying population.

Herzog and Sudia (1973) suggested that yet another type of error has often been made in this area of research. They defined it as "the erroneous belief that available evidence is adequate to support a firm and generalizable conclusion" (p. 213). Furthermore, they suggested that the relevant evidence available at the time was so fragmentary that it constituted "almost a projective device inviting the imposition of form and structure dictated by the predispositions of the analyst rather than by the data" (p. 213). The occurrence of this kind of premature conclusion is likely to be one major reason why experts disagree.

Another related reason for the discrepancy between experts' conclusions relates to the way they make and disseminate generalizations about their findings in a particular area. Research comes from different disciplines, which use different methods and different research strategies. Many writers make primary use of their own observations, or their "clinical experience." For example, Luepnitz (1978) described Goldstein, Freud, and Solnit's (1973) book, *Beyond the Best Interests of the Child,* as a "most extreme view of the adverse effects of separation and divorce." Luepnitz pointed out that the authors cited few empirical studies and did not mention major critiques and exhaustive reviews that were inconsistent with their view.

However, articles purporting to be a review of research may be misleading. Brief reviews are typically done at the beginning of research articles. Additionally, there are *narrative reviews,* which are primarily critical summaries and reviews of literature. Narrative reviews on the impact of father absence have been common since the 1940s. Originally, these reviews were simply chronologically arranged verbal descriptions of research. As the psychological literature grew, reviewers classified studies in contingency tables both by type and by whether outcomes reached statistical significance (Glass, McGaw, & Smith, 1981). This type of review should have located most, if not all, of the relevant literature.

When we (Stevenson & Black, 1988) reviewed the literature on sex-typing, an attempt was made to retrieve every available study that used a two-group comparison between father-absent and father-present children on a measure of sex-typing. Numerous computerized literature searches and exhaustive hand searches of abstracting services and review bibliographies were completed. The final sample included 67 studies, of which 29 were unpublished dissertations.

To establish how comprehensive past summaries have been, the studies cited in each narrative review or discussion of the sex-typing literature were checked against the sample generated by our search. Because reviews were published at different times and the publication process itself is often time-consuming, we computed the proportion of available studies cited in each review based on the date of the most recent study that was cited. For example, although published in 1982, a review by Bourduin and Hengeller was held responsible only for articles available through 1978 because the most recent paper it cited was dated 1978.

Using this procedure, we found that reviewers cited an average of approximately 40 percent of the extant literature. Biller (1974) proved to be the most comprehensive, citing 66 percent of the available literature. Admittedly, some of these reviews were not intended to be comprehensive, and many reviewers do not search for unpublished dissertations. However, many past reviews have omitted generally available literature. This selective citation may well contribute to differing conclusions.

We suggest that, whenever possible, extensive reviews of the literature make use of a technique called meta-analysis. Meta-analysis allows a reviewer to summarize the findings of individual studies that employed different measures and samples. Meta-analyses are used to make sense of bodies of apparently inconsistent literature and to clarify what future research is needed (Schmidt, 1992).

Most meta-analyses differ from narrative reviews because they require two elements: first, an exhaustive search of the literature and, second, a statistical analysis combining all available studies and taking into consideration variables that differed between but not within studies. For example, if some studies used the middle class and others the lower class, information could be obtained about this variable.

Meta-analyses of research comparing children whose parents have divorced with children whose parents have not divorced use a statistic called d. This estimate of effect size is simply the difference between the means of the two groups, divided by a standard deviation (Light & Pillemer, 1984). The d statistic allows us to make statements about the magnitude of differences. As a result, we can compare the magnitude of differences between the two groups across content areas in order to assess differences in cognitive functioning and adjustment or between boys and girls, for example.

The accepted convention concerning effect sizes is that a d of .2 represents a small effect, a d of .5 is a medium effect, and a d of .8 is a large effect (Cohen, 1977). Using this standard, most sex differences in abilities or in personality characteristics are in the small to medium range, whereas sex differences in physical attributes (e.g., how fast a ball is thrown) are "large." Later chapters describe some meta-analyses showing that most of the differences between offspring of divorced and never-divorced parents are also in the small to medium range.

Overview

Experts are influenced by assumptions implicit in society as well as by the schematic thinking prevalent in their discipline. Ferri (1976) suggested that the effects attributed to the one-parent family are based less on evidence than on the assumption that one parent cannot adequately perform a role that society allocates to two. Pleck (1981) showed how what he considered to be anomalous findings were reinterpreted to be consistent with the deficit model. Measures are criticized if they do not produce results that fit researchers' expectations, but escape criticism when they do produce the expected outcomes.

Others (e.g., Adams, 1973) have made the explicit argument that families other than traditional ones are capable of effective functioning. As this view becomes better known, it will influence the interpretation of ambiguous data and the development of research and theory.

Summary

- Researchers have used a variety of methods to study the effects of divorce. These include case-studies and in-depth interviews, simple group comparisons, and process-oriented designs.
- When designing studies, researchers must make a variety of choices. Most have focused on potentially negative effects of divorce because these are consistent with cultural beliefs as well as with psychological theories. Some focus on short-term effects, whereas others look for long-term effects. Other choices concern the selection of measures and samples.
- Generalizations about the effects of divorce must be made with care. They are likely to be accurate when they apply only to specific subgroups.
- Experts studying the effects of divorce sometimes disagree because research findings are inconsistent. In addition, some rely too heavily on their own clinical experience or on misleading literature reviews. Meta-analyses are particularly helpful in dealing with these problems.

The Divorce Process
and Stress

Preview

The most stressful situations that occur in our lives concern the loss of important emotional attachments. On a six-level scale (American Psychiatric Association, 1987), six being the most stressful, divorce is considered level four, being slightly less stressful than the death of one or both parents. Although we tend to focus upon the child's loss of parental relationships as the major stressor in divorce, other losses are involved, also. This chapter considers some of these stressors and how offspring of divorce cope.

Divorce as a Stressor

The divorce process leads to inevitable changes in offsprings' relationships with people to whom they are emotionally attached. These changes may be felt as losses and thus be stressful. Attachments occur not only to people but also to places and even to routines. Accordingly, forced change requires dealing with these emotional losses and a new view of the world. Offspring may be shaken when parents divorce because they are no longer sure that the world is secure and predictable. In addition, even life changes that do not threaten our expectations constitute stressors because they require an adjustment in our cognitive input. For example, children may need to adjust to new siblings or to new schools.

Change is stressful even when it is desirable, such as in graduating from school, trading for a new car, or marrying. This loss of the old, which is essential to go on to the new, may cause stress. If we have been doing well in our old life, we are probably attached to it and will experience loss: we leave behind friends or teachers or positive experiences.

Although stressors differ in intensity, the losses and stresses associated with divorce are similar to those associated with other difficulties in life. Familiarity with the divorce experience may contribute to the understanding of stress and of coping. Significantly, a single stressor is unlikely to result in distress requiring psychological or psychiatric intervention. If several stressors exist concurrently and are then followed by discord, then adjustment problems are more likely (Rutter, 1979).

Many transitions or life event stressors, like divorce, extend over time and require a series of adaptations. Divorce is not just a one-time event but a process that brings about additional challenges and opportunities. Therefore, it is appropriate to refer to the "divorce process."

Following divorce, parents typically live in two different places. As a result, holiday and birthday celebrations may change. Summer vacations may be spent in two locations. Major transition points, such as graduation from high school, require attention and decisions. One child of divorce expressed the following goal for graduation: that parents and their new spouses attend the ceremony and the party afterward. Most importantly, though, the adolescent wanted to be able to talk freely, have a good time, and not be concerned that someone would become angry or say something nasty about the other adults involved. This would seem to be a minimal family goal following divorce. Another major life transition point is that of the offspring's marriage. Whose name is in the newspaper announcement of the engagement or on the invitations? Which father gives you away? Where do you seat the parents? Who gives the parties? How do you arrange people in the pictures? Do you have to worry about arguments and about keeping people apart? Unfortunately, couples about to be married may well wonder why they must worry about these concerns and have old fears renewed about the ramifications of marriage itself.

Divorce often changes offsprings' lives in other ways as well, sometimes as a result of financial problems that follow separation and divorce. Both parents may move if they cannot afford to maintain the previous house. A mother not previously employed may now seek work for pay. Peterson (1989) found that some women adjusted to a diminished income by working more hours. Men, too, may find it necessary to work more or even to take another job.

Issues at these times exist not only for those children for whom both parents have maintained a relationship, but also for children whose noncustodial parent has withdrawn, either dramatically or gradually, from the child's life. That is, some children face the stress of nonexistent parental interaction, whereas others face the stress of trying to balance interactions with two parents.

Clearly, required adaptation following divorce does not occur just at one time. Changes brought about by divorce may have immediate and long-term consequences.

Separation

At some point after making the decision to divorce, one of the partners will usually leave the present family home. Only rarely do couples remain living together until the legal dissolution. This may occur because they are getting along well and wish to continue living together for financial reasons. At other times, each parent in a custody battle has been advised not to leave the house and the advantage that this offers.

Children learn about the end of their parents' marriage in a variety of ways. A national study of over 300 children whose parents had separated or divorced showed that some had frequently discussed separation, whereas others had done so only occasionally. About half of this sample had experienced one or more temporary separations before the final decisive one. However, about one third of these families had not even considered separation until the decision was made and announced by one partner (Furstenberg et al., 1983). This study is congruent with two others that indicate that many children have no reason to expect an end to their parents' marriage. Johnston and Campbell (1988) found that about one-third was aware that a breakup might occur, whereas another third realized that their parents were not getting along. The study also found, however, that many had no knowledge of the impending divorce. The California Children of Divorce study, too, found that at least one-third of the children had only a brief awareness of the parents' unhappiness (Wallerstein & Kelly, 1980).

Life Story

Gene Hackman

At age 58, actor Gene Hackman recalled learning of his parents' impending divorce: "I was just 13, but that Saturday morning is still so vivid. I was playing down the street from our house when I saw my father drive by and give me a light wave of his hand. Somehow, I knew that gesture meant he was going away forever. . . . I hadn't realized anything was wrong. So his leaving came as a shock. It made an incredible impression on what I felt strength and honesty really are."

In 1970 when he was 40 years of age, Hackman decided to seek out his father to tell him of his anger and that he considered his father to have been weak and dishonest. Hackman also asked why his father hadn't stopped to say goodbye. "He refused to discuss what had happened and why he'd left." Hackman finally decided not to expect his father to change and that he still wanted to have a relationship. They did spend time together for the next five years, until his father died.

Hackman doubts that he would have been so sensitive to human behavior, and as good an actor, if he hadn't witnessed his father's departure: "if I hadn't realized how much one small gesture can mean." He also attributes much of his work ethic to feelings about his father. "I was trying to make up for what I perceived as my father's failures. For me, acting was a form of compensation for that early loss, a way of venting my feelings about not having a father."

(*Parade,* February 26, 1989, pp. 10–12.)

As these studies show, some children will be in an extended period of anxiety and confusion regarding a divorce's possible impact to the family, whereas others must deal with a sudden and dramatic announcement. Studies agree that parents are less likely to inform younger children. The reasons for this are unclear. Perhaps, thinking that younger children won't understand, divorcing parents attempt to protect them. Perhaps older children are more likely to notice what is happening and to ask questions. This is most likely true when there has been conflict.

Interparental Conflict

Even when parents have been living separate lives with considerable lack of interaction, conflict often escalates prior to the decision to divorce, and there may be considerable hostility and overt acrimony.

When Luepnitz (1979) asked college students whose parents had divorced to describe the worst part of it, they cited the marital conflict preceding the divorce. Such conflict varies in nature, and ranges from hostile silences and noninteraction, through verbal shouting matches, to physical violence. Many studies of the effects of parental conflict do not separate out the nature of the conflict, but rather have the offspring (or sometimes the parents) rate the degree of conflict on a continuous rating scale.

Wallerstein and Kelly (1980) reported that generally, "There was a good deal of anger, resulting in physical abuse—usually by men of their wives—or property destruction, accompanied by a good deal of fear" (p. 14). The National Study (Furstenberg et al., 1983) found that more than half of dissolved marriages had been characterized by frequent fighting. One in five of those who fought reported having been seriously injured or abused at least once. Johnston and Campbell (1988) found that when instances of aggression occurred, children were present about two-thirds of the time.

The effects of interparental conflict, in varying amounts, upon child adjustment have been studied both for never-divorced and for divorced families. Generally, parental conflict increases the likelihood of behavioral problems and of adjustment difficulty for children. This is true for families with both presently and formerly married parents (Emery, 1982; Jouriles, Pfiffner, & O'Leary, 1988; Long & Forehand, 1987; Long, Forehand, Fauber, & Brody, 1987; O'Leary & Emery, 1984; Shaw & Emery, 1987). Thus, children whose parents remain together during conflict are not spared from negative emotional reactions, nor will a divorce remove the child from a stressful environment if the conflict persists.

This effect seems to hold for a variety of populations and ages, but may be influenced by other variables. The effect of parental conflict is more harmful for those who have previously experienced parental divorce (Fauber, Forehand, Thomas, & Wierson, 1990; Forehand, Brody, Long, Slotkin, & Fauber, 1986). This finding, which has been reported for adolescents, may result from their former experience with conflict due to separation or divorce; that is, they may be sensitized to conflict renewal.

It seems obvious that parental conflict will be stressful for offspring. However, any marital relationship will inevitably include some disagreement and anger. Since adults cannot be expected at all times to hide such conflict from their children, what are the aspects of conflict that are upsetting? What kinds of reactions will children have?

Cummings, Vogel, Cummings, and El-sheikh (1989) interviewed children between 4 and 9 years of age who had viewed videotaped depictions of adult men and women interacting in various ways. The scenes included nonverbal anger, verbal disagreement, hostile disagreement, and affection. The disagreements were sometimes resolved and sometimes not. Children responded negatively to any unresolved expression of anger, including the nonverbal holding back of anger. Male children were more likely than females to become angry and hostile when they viewed adult anger. Based upon these results, we might well predict that, following a divorce (during which there is almost inevitably some unresolved anger), young males are likely to react with some aggressive behaviors. In this study, the reported distress was greater for children from those homes in which there had been interparent physical aggression, perhaps because these children had previously seen unresolved anger escalate into physical violence.

For those who want to help children adjust to divorce, the message is clear: Adjustment will be hastened if the parents can resolve issues and eliminate conflict, including the conflict indicated by hostile silence. Parents may be unaware that their children perceive such conflict and that it distresses them. Significantly, research shows that adolescents prefer to live in a one-parent home rather than in a two-parent home that is high in conflict (McLoughlin & Whitfield, 1984).

General Life Changes

Conventional wisdom advises that there should be as few changes as possible for children of divorce. Is this view justified? Elkind (1986) has suggested that either parental divorce or moving is a major stressor for children. As previously noted, though, only when there are several concurrent stressors along with family discord is there likely to be a problem. Of course, any change constitutes a stress. Changes require mental energy to deal with new events; some changes are stressful because they involve the loss of the familiar or people to whom there is attachment, albeit at a level lower than that for parents. This suggests that some changes that would ordinarily be readily dealt with may be more difficult at the time of divorce. Examples of potentially stressful changes include changes in housing, in schools, in child care arrangements, or the loss of friends from school or neighborhood.

Stirtzinger (1986) found that children who had moved from the family home after divorce showed a discrete longing for it. In fact, this group thought more about the loss of the family home than of a parental figure. Interestingly, Stirtzinger and Cholvat (1990) found that preschool-aged children who evidenced high attachment to their former homes or objects in them, were rated by parents and teachers as having better behavioral adjustment. It is not clear if this kind of response serves as a coping mechanism or whether such reactions would also help the adjustment of older children. It does remind us, though, that some people facing the same external situation seem to handle it better than others. Beardsall and Dunn (1992) interviewed families having one 8- and one 6-year-old. They found that, although over two-thirds of the children had negative experiences that could be expected to have moderate to severe impact, a majority of the siblings reacted differently to the stress.

Economic Stresses

The median income for families headed by one person is less than for two-parent families, even when child support is paid. This is especially true for families headed by women. In 1990, the median income for single women with children was $13,100, but the median income for married couples with children was three times that amount, $41,300 (Ahlburg & DeVita, 1992). In reviewing the effects of father absence, Herzog and Sudia (1973) found that when the socioeconomic factor was taken into consideration, detrimental effects of divorce were often reduced or eliminated. This may be an indirect effect in that the amount of decline in income is a predictive factor for women's adjustment following divorce (Braver, Gonzalez, Sandler, & Wolchik, 1985).

Desimone-Luis, O'Mahoney, and Hunt (1979) found that children who showed severe behavioral problems following divorce were living in family units that had experienced a severe drop in income immediately following the separation. (A severe drop in income was defined as approximately half the previous income.) In other words, the adolescent whose parents had previously owned a summer home and who wore only expensive, brand label clothing might be as distressed as someone who had much less but who had not previously enjoyed an expensive lifestyle.

In addition to the actual financial problems associated with living in a single-parent family, some children will face the stress of arguments between the parents about whether the amount of support is justified, or whether the custodial parent is using the money appropriately.

■_____

Life Story

Will

Although Will's parents, Allen and Kaye, separated when he was 4 years old, the official divorce did not occur until 5 years later. Will's parents were trade school graduates who grew up in a steel mill area of

Pennsylvania. Will was the oldest child of this marriage, but he had half-siblings from his mother's prior marriage. Some fighting prior to the separation occurred behind shut doors; unfortunately, at the time Will believed that his parents were fighting over him and perhaps his younger brother. Later arguments, after separation, were clearly over child support.

At the time of separation and later conflict, Will's reaction was to retire to his room and cry. He is not sure about his reasoning, but thinks that his desire to control situations beyond his command led to his avoiding interactions with peers. He also had difficulty concentrating. This, though, might have been due to a diagnosed hyperactivity. In spite of these problems, Will and his siblings have all earned high grades in school.

After the separation, Will's mother often worked three jobs to support her four boys. Will learned to do his own laundry at the age of 5; at 6 he began to cook for the family, while the other children did most of the cleaning. The children saw their father every weekend, until sometime during adolescence when, by their own choice, the boys reduced interaction. This was in part because of the boys' involvement in athletics, in part because, as soon as possible, each worked to help support the family, and in part because of their anger at Allen, who had gone back to court on numerous occasions—more times than Will can remember—asking that child support be stopped or reduced. In adolescence Will was subjected to sexual abuse from one of his mother's boyfriends at a time when his mother was in the hospital. Will did not want to tell his mother what was happening, as she was already so burdened. During this time he became suicidal and began to drink until he was drunk. After several months he did "explode," stop the abuse, and reveal what was happening. At the same time, he seemed to have a change in behavior generally and became interactive with others at school. He also decided that he would not in the future use alcohol when stressed about something. He has held to this and now deliberately thinks about problems, trying also to talk to someone about them.

Allen has not paid support for higher education for any of the boys, all of whom went to major universities. Will, who is now 20 years old and a junior in college, has not talked to his father for four years. On his sixteenth birthday, Will's father took him out in the afternoon and brought him home 12 hours later without having fed him and without saying goodbye to him. Will invited his father to his high school graduation and party, but Allen replied that he was "too busy" to come. In contrast, although Will rarely saw his mother after entering college, he feels that she is his best friend because of her efforts, both financially and emotionally, to support him and his siblings. Although he found the idea of her dating to be somewhat upsetting when he was younger, he is delighted that his mother has a fiancé with whom she has been living for a year, and Will considers this man to be his "dad."

Will presently works at odd jobs to support himself through school. Sometimes he thinks that he wants to become a doctor, and sometimes an engineer. At present, Will is in the top 10 percent of his university class.

Will believes that a fear of commitment grows directly out of the conflict between his parents over the years. This fear arises from a past pattern in which he too quickly becomes attached to someone he is seeing. For this reason he dates seldom and casually, as he does not wish to marry until later. He will insist on cohabitation prior to marriage. Will is aware that it is not a good idea to avoid conflict at all costs as he does, and is working on changing his pattern of holding in discontent until he explodes in anger. On the positive side, he is proud of his self-reliance and ability to cope with finances. He does not concern himself with worrying about whether others approve of his clothing, or even of his actions. He does believe that he would have been better off if he had seen a professional to talk about the divorce; he certainly believes that he should have seen someone earlier about the sexual abuse, rather than having to deal with this on his own.

In spite of his experiences with his father, Will believes that, ideally, when divorce does occur, joint custody would enable the children to see both parents as much as possible.

Coping with Divorce

As shown, divorce brings an inevitable need to cope with a variety of life changes. The literature (Dubow & Tisak, 1989) shows that stressful life events at a given time are likely to be associated with academic difficulties and general behavior problems, but that measures of accumulated stressful events over time and present adjustment are not related. This means that there are coping mechanisms, or buffers, that can be used by individuals.

Inevitably, offspring will cope with the stress of parental divorce in different ways. Younger children may use strategies different from those of other children because they are less competent in the use of some of them. For example, Scherman and Lepak (1986) reported that children in early as compared to late elementary school were more defensive about the idea of parental separation.

The literature suggests four coping responses that might be used in dealing with the stresses resulting from divorce: changing belief systems, finding social support, using social problem-solving skills, and avoidance. Because children's behavior and adjustment is related to that of their parents, we provide examples for both offspring and parents.

Changing Belief Systems

Each person's definition of who is in his or her family differs. When Klee, Schmidt, and Johnson (1989) asked children who was in their family, some children included only those living in the same house with them. As they grew older, many began to include both biological and stepkin who lived in other places. In one study (Isaacs, Leon, & Kline, 1987) children between 4 and 12 years of age whose parents were divorced were asked to "draw a picture of your family." Both biological parents were more likely to be included in the picture when there was joint custody, frequent visitation, and when parents got along with each other.

Kurdek, Blisk, and Siesky (1981) suggest that the beliefs children hold about family life influence their adjustment to divorce. Feelings of loss may require the understanding that families can continue even when parents live apart, and that one can have more than one home. Anger on the part of children will dissipate more rapidly if they accept that parents have the right to happiness in their own lives and that for their particular parents, this cannot happen together. Children may feel cared for rather than abandoned if they are told that parents are divorcing because, "We fight too much when we are together, and we have decided to separate because our fighting is not good for you children."

Adults who feel that divorce is shameful may be depressed for a longer period of time. Conversely, adults who believe that the divorce is better for the children, or who know that there was nothing they could do to avoid it, may be better able to avoid or stop guilt reactions. Intervention programs sometimes are directed to changing these beliefs.

■─────────────────────────────

Life Story

Shirley
Shirley, an 11-year-old girl, wrote the following poem toward the end of her parents' marriage:

> We rake the leaves from the trees
> We shovel the snow from the sky

all we do when people we love fight

Is go to our room and cry.

When her father found this he became angry. Her interpretation at the time was that she was not supposed to be upset, and that she was not to talk about this. She was a "good girl" and tried to do what was expected. As a young college adult, her present view is that her father was bothered because she was upset. However, she still has considerable difficulty acknowledging her negative emotions or talking about them with others.

Social Support

Social support refers to the existence of people and experiences that lead the individual to believe that he or she is cared for, loved, esteemed, and valued. Studies of social support for children have typically dealt with support from relatives, teachers, and friends rather than from parents.

A variety of studies have demonstrated that people deal more successfully with stressful life events when they have more available social support (e.g., Dubow & Tisak, 1989). Those individuals who actively go to friends to talk about the situation, who accept sympathy from friends, or who seek reassurance from relatives exhibit this coping skill.

Social Problem-Solving Skills

Social problem-solving skills imply a fairly active approach to dealing with life's frustrations. This may involve thinking about and trying a variety of approaches on your own or seeking information from others. Kurdek (1981) hypothesized that possessing such skills would likely result in better adjustment.

Avoidance

The fourth frequently used method of coping with stress is to block it out of your mind and avoid dealing with it. Nonproductive avoidance includes sleeping a lot, watching TV, or using alcohol or other drugs. However, some other avoidance behaviors may be more useful. College students have reported that after parental divorce, rather than finding themselves distracted in the classroom, many had instead successfully "buried themselves in schoolwork." Others might involve themselves in extracurricular activities (Black, 1982). Wallerstein and Kelly (1980) reported that adolescents typically spent a lot of time with their peers, an activity that might be motivated in part by avoidance of the family situation.

If the divorce has produced a feeling of betrayal, people may simply avoid relationships altogether. As Jones, Cohn, and Miller (1991, p. 118) have noted, "The ultimate protection against betrayal is to have no relationships, or only superficial ones." This reaction of fearing or avoiding future romantic relationships might be the response either of a former spouse, or of an offspring who observed betrayal.

These four coping strategies might be used in dealing with the stress of parental divorce. However, we should not automatically assume that their use is healthy. The acceptance of some beliefs (e.g., that "men cannot be trusted") may lead to problems. Continually seeking comfort and reassurance from others does not inevitably result in resolution of real issues. Attempting to solve the problem of maintaining a relationship with a parent who has withdrawn may result only in frustration. Avoidance of thinking about issues may be workable only in the short run. By trial and error, many offspring of divorce find a combination of strategies to cope successfully with the stress of divorce. Others require help.

Overview

The losses associated with parental separation and the divorce process have psychological consequences like those of other kinds of losses. Nonetheless, families will differ in the kind of losses, with some experiencing the loss of physical places, and some losing actual relationships. Most will experience the stress of a change in economic resources, and some an actual drop into poverty.

Individuals will differ in the support available in their environment, the extent to which they can handle stress, and the means by which they attempt to do so.

We have suggested four coping strategies that might be used in dealing with the stress of parental divorce. However, one should not automatically assume that their use is healthy.

Summary

- The parental divorce process can be viewed as a series of stressors that are related to inevitable changes in the lives of offspring.
- Offsprings' reactions to the departure of a parent are related to their awareness and understanding of the impending divorce.
- Interparental conflict causes distress in offspring regardless of whether the parents ultimately divorce and particularly when children feel responsible for the conflict.

- Multiple, simultaneous changes in children's lives increase their level of stress, particularly when they are accompanied with family discord.
- Economic stress may account for some of what we typically refer to as "the effects of divorce."
- Divorce will have different effects upon different children, even in the same family and facing the same things, partly because different people use different mechanisms for coping with stress.

Family Relationships

Preview

Divorce results in changes in family structure. As discussed in the last chapter offspring may cope with their parents' divorce by altering their conception of families. In this chapter we consider the impact of custody decisions, parental functioning after divorce, and the relationships among family members.

Characteristics of Divorced Parents

The end of a marriage can affect partners in a variety of ways: changes in sleeping patterns, eating habits, daily habits, and self-image; and problems with interpersonal relationships (e.g., Huddleston & Hawkings, 1986). Not surprisingly, persons who are separated or divorced are more likely to be psychiatric patients, to become physically ill, and to be alcoholic. They are more likely to die from suicide or homicide and to have car accidents (Bloom, Asher, & White, 1978; Magura & Shapiro, 1988; Somers, 1979; Verbrugge, 1979).

Why are these separated or divorced adults different from those who are married? The two possible explanations are not mutually exclusive. The first refers to a hypothesis regarding a pre- and postmarital disability. According to it, certain people have always had a psychological disability, although marriage may mask it temporarily. This explanation hypothesizes that divorced people are more likely to exhibit behavioral and personality disorders, and that these disorders probably contribute to divorce. For example, people with alcohol and gambling addictions and those who have difficulty maintaining employment may be more likely to divorce. The second hypothesis is that any group subjected to high stress will be temporarily less able to function adequately. Supporting this interpretation are findings that show a decrease in ability to function among persons whose spouse has died (e.g., Stroebe & Stroebe, 1983). The extra demands of single parenting are stressful and may help lead to the greater personal distress reported by single, as compared to married, mothers (Cohen, 1983).

The ending of a marital relationship for any reason is stressful. Divorce means that losses are occurring for the adults as well as for the children. For most parents, these include a reduction in the amount of time spent with children. Other important losses include a loved person (for at least one partner), a changed view of life's possibilities, and losses of property, income, some friends, and persons who have been considered relatives. Perhaps as important as anything in our society, we view the ideal marriage as a place where we are accepted and where we enjoy psychological support. Whether this has in fact occurred, the single person must now face that it cannot presently be expected. Some proportion of separating adults must also deal with betrayal, a "serious violation of the norms and expectations of a relationship." Research findings (Jones, Cohn, & Miller, 1991) show that, for adults, the most common betrayal comes from marital partners. Among women, betrayal due to a husband's extramarital affair is more common than any other type.

Because of these factors, divorcing parents will have emotional reactions similar to those described for the offspring. They will feel grief at the loss of a relationship that they had expected to work. Anger, too, is common and may be a stage that is necessary in order to stop the caring and sorrow. Many are fearful about the likelihood of ever finding another relationship. In addition, there is anxiety about economic problems. Some are embarrassed to admit to family or colleagues that they are divorced. Often parents feel guilt or anger about the possible effects of divorce upon the children.

There may also be differences between the long-term psychological consequences of divorce for fathers and mothers. We have previously noted that women may be more affected economically. Wallerstein (1985a) has reported that ten years after divorce, there were significant differences between formerly married men and women in quality of life and in psychological recovery, with the women doing less well. These women, less often remarried, reported both more anger and more widespread loneliness. Moreover, Wijnberg and Holmes (1992) found that a woman's adaptation to divorce was related to the meaning and value she attached to the mothering component of her role and to the comfort she felt in accepting a work identity.

As was noted earlier, some people divorce repeatedly. Research with physicians who were studied over a 20-year period showed that the multiply-divorced differed from others in that they tended to exhibit greater nonconforming, impulsive, and risk-taking tendencies in general, as well as a greater likelihood of negative health practices such as cigarette smoking (McCranie & Kahan, 1986).

Sometimes temporarily and sometimes permanently, divorced parents are likely to have problems meeting all of the responsibilities of healthy parenting. Houses may not be kept clean; bedtime and mealtime routines may disappear; homework may not be checked. Children may in general not be supervised, and parents may be more critical and less positive. That is, a divorce indirectly affects a child's well-being when it results in pressures upon a parent who is then depressed or unable to cope (e.g., Colletta, 1983). One way to help the children of divorce is to help their parents function well psychologically.

Mothering, Fathering, and Custody

A father asking for custody once commented to one of the authors, "I've been both a mother and a father to those children since they were born." When asked what this meant, he replied that he had always participated in basic caretaking tasks such as changing diapers and putting his children to bed, and that he felt as strongly about them as did their mother. Perhaps this view was the basis for a newspaper story a few years ago reporting on a young girl whose winning Mother's Day entry had nominated her divorced and custodial father.

The only way in which mothers and fathers are inherently different is that they are female or male. Does this affect what they can do as parents, and should this distinction be relevant when custody decisions are made? Both fathers and mothers can provide basic needs, emotional nurture, and socialization for their children. Nonetheless, society has often assumed that the major job of a father was to "provide for" his family, and that the major job of a mother was to supply daily care and affection. Now, however, most families are dependent upon the income of both parents. Both mothers and fathers have involved themselves in socialization, although they have differed in the amount of direct parent-child interaction.

Certainly both men and women can parent. Greif (1990) suggested that there are many unsubstantiated myths about single fathers. He argued that they are not extraordinary men but simply fathers who, for a variety of reasons, end up with custody. Perhaps more importantly, he suggested that, "Their successes are even more gratifying and encouraging, because they show that with little previous training men can adapt to raising their children alone" (p. 43).

When research is done on this question, it is important to consider the sex and age of the child, because folk wisdom suggests that young males especially need their fathers after a certain age. In line with this, Maccoby, Depner, and Mnookin (1988) reported that parents frequently mentioned that fathers can exercise better control over older boys. Fathers may feel more strongly about one sex than the other. For example, Hetherington, Cox, and Cox (1982) reported that fathers were more likely to sustain visitation with a boy than with a girl.

Whether parental role models are necessary for optimal development, it is possible for father-custody and mother-custody families to differ, yet both be appropriate places to rear children.

Sex of Parent

Should the sex of the parent and of the child be considered in making custody determinations? The view that children function better in the custody of a same-sex parent is still popular, yet Warshak (1987) suggested, without empirical evidence, that there is a general societal prejudice against custodial fathers. With the exception of a few small-scale studies (e.g., Furstenberg & Zill, 1984), research comparing offspring in mother-custody and father-custody single-parent families typically finds no differences in outcome, or that small differences disappear or reverse when remarriage occurs (Downey & Powell, 1993; Fidler & Saunders, 1988; Santrock & Warshak, 1979; Santrock, Warshak, & Elliott, 1981; Schnayer & Orr, 1989; Warshak & Santrock, 1983a,b; Warshak, 1987).

Furthermore, evidence concerning the advantages of a same-sex custodial parent runs counter to same-sex expectations (Downey & Powell, 1993). It is therefore reasonable not to support an a priori preference for mother-custody.

The sex of the custodial parent is probably only indirectly related to outcomes because of its relation to parental conflict, parenting skill, and financial status. These considerations are undoubtedly more directly influential (Warshak & Santrock, 1983a,b; Warshak, 1986). In addition, the matter of sex of the custodial parent is confounded with a variety of variables, including why the parent has custody, the extent to which the custody decision was contested, and changes in physical custody.

As is often true, more research in this area is needed. However, it is reasonable to conclude that the sex of the parent should not take precedence over issues of parenting ability or of attachment.

Joint Custody

As a result of either agreement or a court hearing, minor children will end up either with one parent having sole custody or with the parents having joint custody. Originally, joint custody was preferred because of the expectation that both parents were more likely to remain involved in child rearing, and that this would improve adjustment among offspring, resulting in less re-litigation. One of the major questions still to be resolved concerns whether or when joint custody is to be preferred (Sales, Manber, & Rohman, 1992).

It is important to distinguish between legal custody and physical custody. For example, a child may live with her mother and have regular visitation with her father, yet either parent could legally give consent for medical treatment. Most instances of joint custody refer to legal custody; spending equal time with each parent is relatively rare.

The literature on joint custody is difficult to interpret. Many of the studies have not differentiated between joint legal and physical custody, and early studies were often based upon samples who had voluntarily chosen this arrangement because of their desire to do what they felt was best for the child. Not surprisingly, conclusions appear to differ depending upon these and other variables.

Children of divorce prefer joint custody (Luepnitz, 1982), and college students say that they believe this is the fairest arrangement (K. R. Kelly, personal communication, 1992). Joint custody is more likely to keep both parents involved in child rearing (Arditti, 1992; Lowery, 1986; Johnston, Kline, & Tschann, 1989), perhaps because there are responsibilities and rights. Conversely, perhaps those parents who are likely to be irresponsible do not seek joint custody.

The view of parents concerning joint custody is mixed. Parents who would probably not have had custody tend to be positive about this arrangement (Arditti, 1992), whereas those who think that they should have sole custody tend to dislike joint custody, a situation with less individual power. In general, fathers will be more positive about joint custody than mothers. There is no particular reason to believe that joint custody will, in itself, either reduce or increase interpersonal or legal conflicts (Donnelly & Finklehor, 1992; Sales, Manber, & Rohman, 1992).

Although offspring and some parents prefer joint custody, is it really in the best interest of the offspring? Early studies of small samples found either that children were better adjusted in this situation or that they were no worse. These studies employed samples of families with parents who had voluntarily chosen joint custody because they believed it was best for the children. One study comparing children in joint custody, single custody, and non-divorced families showed that children in joint custody were as well or better off, especially in their feelings about relationships with fathers and mothers (Glover & Steele, 1989). In contrast, Donnelly and Finklehor (1992) found no evidence that children in shared custody arrangements had better or less conflictive relationships with their parents. Recent studies have also included families who did not choose joint custody but who had it imposed upon them. For example, Kline, Tschann, Johnston, and Wallerstein (1989) concluded that joint physical custody, in which children spent largely equal amounts of time with each parent, did not affect adjustment.

Children in joint custody are overrepresented in those groups who are the best off or the worst off (Johnston, Kline, & Tschann, 1989; Buchanan, et al., 1991). They are doing better than most when their parents are cooperating or co-parenting. If the parents continue to have extensive and overt battles and involve the children, then these children are the worst off (Johnston, Kline, & Tschann, 1989).

Detrimental effects for some offspring may be the result of forced interaction, resulting in conflict, between the divorced parents. Parents who do not enter joint custody entirely willingly may still be able to avoid conflict and thus find the arrangement workable. Further, a recent study (Buchanan, Maccoby, & Dornbusch, 1991) has concluded that it is not parental conflict that results in maladjustment on the part of adolescent children, but rather whether the children feel responsible for attempting to keep peace between their parents. This is one finding from the Stanford Child Custody Study, a longitudinal study of various sorts of custody and living arrangements described in Maccoby, Depner, and Mnookin (1988).

The National Survey study (Furstenberg, 1988) found that only a minority of those parents with physical custody felt that the other parent was assuming a fair share of responsibility. Furstenberg and his colleagues refer to the "inside" parent with whom a child lives and the "outside" parent who is visited. The level of involvement by the outside parent is related to geographical distance and to the extent to which child support is being paid. It is likely that the lack of financial support is associated both with an outside parent who tends to avoid interaction and with an inside parent who tends to refuse interaction. However, generally only a fraction of the parents who have physical custody of a child give the outside parent influence in important decisions concerning the child.

Even when parents have joint physical custody, they do little consultation with one another (Ahrons, 1981; Steinman, 1981). Ahrons reported that this results from attempts to avoid conflict. Camara and Resnick (1988) make a distinction between interparental conflict and parental cooperation, suggesting that low conflict and low cooperation can coexist. It is also possible for couples to be in conflict, to dislike one another personally, and to still carefully work out interactions such as making certain that the children see the other parent and encouraging a good ongoing relationship. Clearly, we need more information about the effects of joint legal and physical custody and the situations in which it is desirable.

Furstenberg and Cherlin (1991) have suggested on the basis of present data that, although there are few reasons to expect differences between the different custody arrangements, our society may wish to presume joint legal custody because this sends a message to fathers, who rarely obtain sole custody, that society respects their rights and that they have responsibilities for children.

Relationships among Members of Divorced Families

Research on a large undergraduate sample with never-divorced parents found that most college students have close relations with both parents (Black, 1985). Although males and females responded similarly, students felt closer to mothers than to fathers. However, this mean difference masks underlying individual differences. About half gave parents the same rating. (Similarly, Fox, Kimmerly, and Schafer, 1991, found that the type of attachment to one parent was dependent upon that to the other.) Of the remainder of the young adults in Black's sample, about 35 percent rated attachment to mothers higher than to fathers, whereas about 15 percent rated fathers higher than mothers.

Using retrospective ratings, Black (1985) also demonstrated that offspring felt closest to parents during elementary school and then after they had left home and least close to parents during junior and senior high school. The respondents largely ascribed the drop in ratings to issues of control that arose during adolescence. The issues concerned such matters as homework, housework, hours, and friends. Relations in college usually improve because the parents no longer attempt to exert control and/or because the offspring realize that the attempts at control are appropriate.

These findings are relevant when assessing the effects of parental divorce upon parent-child relationships. For example, if one is assessing closeness following a divorce or remarriage and the offspring is an adolescent living at home, observed effects might be the result of typical adolescent issues rather than of the divorce.

Life Story

Annabelle

Annabelle is a 23-year-old married female with two young children, a 4 year old and an infant. Annabelle is the middle of three girls. She grew up in the country in a spacious home with a large yard and swimming pool. Her mother, Brenda, a housewife, was there whenever the children wanted her. Her father, Brady, a high school dropout, was primarily the manager of a grocery store department but also often held a second job in order to provide as he wished for his family. Annabelle reports that Brady primarily knows how to show affection through material goods rather than through words. Generally the family was a happy one during Annabelle's early years. Religion was important. There was some stress over the father's two jobs, since he slept a lot when home. A first three-month separation occurred when Annabelle was 13. Several years after a reconciliation, Brady began an affair with a young woman who was a friend of his older daughter. Conflict began between the parents and included some interactions in which Brenda would slap Brady or he would grip her until he left bruises. Annabelle not only viewed these, but she also attempted to stand between her parents to keep them apart. Brenda took the three children, ranging from 14 to 19 years of age, out of town in order to discuss her options with them. They advised divorce. Conflict continued for a brief time and included name-calling and involvement of the children. After the divorce, Brady moved in with his girlfriend, and they married within the year. The two minor children remained with their mother. Although they then had to move to a two-bedroom apartment, Annabelle stayed in the same school district. Dependent upon a high school degree, Brenda went to work as an accounts clerk for a large manufacturing company. Finances were tight. The daughters now prepared dinner and helped with the housework. They talked more to one another and grew closer. Brady saw the children every weekend and called them once or twice a week. Annabelle remembers crying a lot because the changes were so hard on everyone. Both parents allowed the offspring to talk about how they felt. Annabelle's schoolwork continued at the same level, and she had no behavioral problems. Throughout Annabelle's life, people have commented that she was a very sweet person, and this continued even during these changes.

Brady and his younger wife have two children who are about the age of Annabelle's own. Recently, Brenda remarried, and Annabelle now has older stepbrothers with whom she is just becoming acquainted. Annabelle gets along with both stepparents and feels that having children the same age gives her something in common with her stepmother.

Although Annabelle has some regrets that she did not spend much time with her father, she feels that the divorce was the best thing for the entire family, as they no longer had to live with the conflict. Adjustment was helped by the constant presence of Annabelle's mother, her best friend, and by a belief in God.

Annabelle married shortly after high school graduation. Now, she is not only happily married and rearing two children, but also attending college. She values education and thinks that everyone needs a career to fall back on. After she obtains a degree that will enable her to work with abused children, Annabelle would like to work part-time so that she can be home with her children.

Relationships with Parents

Over time, interaction between noncustodial parents and children decreases. College offspring are more likely to have contact with their mothers than with fathers (Cooney, 1985). Although about half of college students talked weekly with their divorced fathers (Cooney, 1985), Furstenberg et al. (1983) found that half of the children in their nationally representative sample had not seen their fathers in the last year. Contact with noncustodial mothers is greater than for fathers

(Furstenberg et al., 1983; Greif & Pabst, 1988; Springer & Wallerstein, 1983; Warshak & Santrock, 1983a,b). Reportedly, lack of contact with the noncustodial parent is often a matter of distress to children.

Using data from the National Survey of Families and Households, Cooney and Uhlenberg (1990) looked at fathers between 50 and 79 years of age and compared those who had divorced and those who hadn't. A divorce was associated with decreased likelihood that these men had an adult child in their house and with fewer general contacts with the now adult children. However, about half of these fathers were in weekly contact with their children, whereas about 90 percent of the never-divorced had contact.

Even when the noncustodial father remains in contact, these parent-child interactions differ from those of fathers in two-parent homes. Amato (1987) reported that noncustodial fathers exhibited less support and less control and punishment. In contrast, single-mother support and punishment did not differ from the two-parent home. The same sample of mother-custody children reported simultaneously more household responsibility and more autonomy. Weiss (1979) observed that children in single-parent families are more likely to be treated as an equal partner by their parents. This includes not only decision-making but also receiving information about family problems.

Studies of children's closeness to mothers after divorce have used the father-absence paradigm, primarily with college students. Only two studies (Fine, Moreland, & Schwebel, 1983; Parish & Kappes, 1980) reported lower ratings for divorced mothers than for married mothers. One (White, Brinkerhoss, & Booth, 1985) reported higher ratings for custodial mothers than for married mothers. The other (Sauer & Fine, 1988) reported lower ratings for noncustodial mothers than for married mothers. None of these differences was large, and other studies (Black, 1985; Peterson & Zill, 1986) found no differences.

All of the studies reported that divorced noncustodial fathers received lower ratings than married fathers. However, the ratings of closeness to custodial fathers did not differ from those for married fathers (Peterson & Zill, 1986; White, Brinkerhoss, & Booth, 1985). One investigation (Orthner, Brown, & Ferguson, 1976) reported that there was an unusual closeness between single-parent fathers and their children. This suggests that it is not the divorce per se that leads to lesser feelings of closeness. Such a view is further supported by the findings that one-third of young adults reported feeling close to their fathers following a divorce (Cooney, Smyer, Hagestad, & Klock, 1986).

In a unique study, Villwock, Peckskamp, and Black (1990), using a multivariate analysis, examined college students' feelings of closeness to fathers. In agreement with previous findings, the overall sample of divorced fathers received lower average closeness ratings than married fathers. However, the two groups of fathers also differed on other measures that might be expected to lead to poorer relationships. These included having affairs, drug or alcohol use, physical abuse, financial support, frequency of contact, trustworthiness, and parent acceptance of child.

In attempting to make sense of what has happened, many children will seek to ascribe blame. This is easier if one parent has exhibited problem behaviors such as alcoholism or gambling, but many parents also will have shown sexual infidelity or already established another relationship at the time of the separation.

Whatever the mediating mechanism, when Villwock et al. (1990) took these variables into consideration using multiple regression, the ratings of closeness to fathers were no longer related to parental marital status. Regardless of parental marital status, offspring felt closer to fathers who were perceived as being accepting, supportive, and trustworthy.

This study suggests that there is no necessary effect of divorce per se upon feelings of family closeness. Differences reported in past research can be attributed to more specific characteristics and behaviors that may be more common among divorced fathers but also occur in never-divorced fathers. Such a conclusion is consistent with the finding that college students from never-divorced unhappy families reported difficult father-child relationships (White et al., 1985).

These findings have implications both for the children and for the fathers. Cooney and Uhlenberg (1990) found a sharply reduced probability that fathers who had ever divorced considered their adult children potential sources of support in times of need. They also found that the degree of actual and expected interaction was associated with the number of children involved. With more children there was greater likelihood that contact would be maintained with at least one.

Many elderly people depend upon their children for care in later years. The offspring of divorce may in fact be less likely to give such care when the past relationship has been unrewarding. Problems for the elderly may be particularly severe when they lack both a new marital partner and friendly relations with their children. The rate of suicide for those over 65 is highest for presently divorced males as compared to those who are married or widowed (Meehan, Saltzman, & Sattin, 1991). It is also possible that the aging of parents will produce further stress for the adult offspring who will, for example, have to decide whether to assist a father who did not earlier assist them.

The usual legal requirement that noncustodial parents have a right to visit minor children reflects an awareness of a parent's rights. However, unless the noncustodial father is emotionally disturbed or there is high conflict between the parents, more frequent visitation may also be related to better adjustment among offspring (Hetherington, Cox, & Cox, 1978; Jacobson, 1978; Lowenstein & Koopman, 1978; Wallerstein & Kelly, 1980). Guidubaldi, Cleminshaw, and Perry (1985) found that elementary school children had better physical health when the child spent more time with the noncustodial parent.

In contrast, Furstenberg, Morgan, and Allison (1987), in analyses of a large scale sample, found few significant relationships between contact and various measures of child adjustment. Some smaller samples have also reported no relationship (e.g., Kurdek & Berg, 1983; Kurdek, Blisk, & Siesky, 1981; Luepnitz, 1982). Hodges, Wechsler, and Ballantine (1979) found that for their sample of preschool-aged children, more frequent visitation was associated with greater overt aggression. Hess and Camara (1979) found that greater visitation duration, not frequency, was positively associated with adjustment. Isaacs, Montalvo, and Abelsohn (1986) concluded that regularity and consistency is more important than frequency.

In divorcing families, the quality of parent-child relationships likely will depend upon a variety of factors, including the outcome-measure considered, the length of time since the divorce, the custody arrangement, the age of the child, the relationship between the parents, and whether or not remarriage has occurred. Although occurring less often than custodial parents may believe, some situations involve abuse or neglect, where continued contact with a noncustodial parent may be harmful or even dangerous for children.

Relationships with Siblings

For siblings in never-divorced families, Black (1985) reported that college undergraduates felt less close to siblings than to parents. In contrast to parent-child relationships, ratings of sibling closeness were not lower in adolescence. However, as with parent-child relationships, the usual pattern was for siblings to feel closest to one another when they no longer lived together.

One consequence of the usual custody and visitation arrangement is that siblings are with one another steadily and for more time than with either parent. They share experiences and may take comfort in facing the unfamiliar together. Siblings use one another as confidants, potentially increasing the feelings of closeness. On the other hand, siblings may make opposing choices. They may assign blame differently for the divorce or even choose to live with different parents. One potentially divisive situation arises when one child is "put in charge" of another. This happens, for example, when a parent needs assistance in child supervision while at work or carrying out household chores.

Although siblings' relationships might be an important resource in helping children to adjust to divorce, they might also be characterized by animosity (Eno, 1985). Hetherington (1989) suggested that post-divorce sibling relationships could be described as positively affectionate, rejecting, enmeshed, or ambivalent.

Amato (1987) reported more conflict among siblings in one-parent families than in never-divorced families. MacKinnon (1988–89) used measures of behavior in a game to compare young children from married and divorced families. At both preschool and elementary school ages, siblings in divorced families had more negative physical and verbal interactions and were more noncompliant with one another. However, there was also more caretaking behavior especially directed toward younger siblings, including attempts to teach and responses to requests for help. Similarly, Summers, Summers, and Ascione (in press) reported that siblings in single-parent families displayed more guidance-related behaviors than those in two-parent families. Consistent with previous conclusions about sex differences at this age, MacKinnon (1988-89) found that those dyads containing older male siblings from families of divorce were more negative. She also noted that the sibling relationship was associated with the quality of the relationship between the ex-spouses.

Zembar, Behrendt, and Etz (1991) found that only 28 percent of their sample from divorced families, presently college undergraduates, had confided in siblings. Over 40 percent said that they argued more after the divorce, whereas slightly more than 30 percent said they argued less. Interestingly, regardless of whether they engaged in arguments, almost 70 percent thought that they had grown closer to their siblings, although almost 17 percent grew more distant. This would suggest that conclusions will depend upon the kind of measure used. Behavioral observations that include arguing and other negative reactions might show fewer good relationships than reports of felt closeness. This same study reported that college students who had a self-reported high quality of sibling relationship were less likely to feel depressed or lonely.

Perhaps it will be necessary not only to consider the kind of measure used but also the developmental stage. Wallerstein (1985b) found that a group who had been in late elementary school or adolescence at the time of divorce developed strong and supportive relationships with their siblings.

Future research should also consider the possibility that relationships between siblings may be affected by a remarriage, and not just by the original divorce.

Relationships in Stepfamilies

The word stepfamily refers to a great variety of family configurations. If both parents remarry, a child will need to deal with four adults in parenting roles, eight or more grandparental figures (if a divorce occurred in that generation), as well as step or half-siblings. One would certainly expect greater difficulty in short-term adjustment when there is a greater number of relationships to negotiate (Clingempeel, 1981; Clingempeel, Ievloi, & Brand, 1984; Pasley & Ihinger-Tallman, 1982). However, this need not result in any differential long-term effects.

One might wonder whether remarriage will affect a child's relationships with the parents of the original family, as has been reported for siblings. In children's drawings of their families, a parental remarriage did not predict the omission of the noncustodial parent (Isaacs, Leon, & Kline, 1987). In addition, Peterson and Zill (1986) found that children felt as close to remarried custodial mothers and fathers as to those who were not remarried. In contrast, White et al. (1985) found that when a mother remarried, the presence of stepsiblings resulted in lower attachment to adults in the household and greater attachment to the absent parent. These comparisons may have been made at different times in the remarriage, and the groups involved were small. Clearly, further research is needed.

Life Story

Mark

Bill and Andrea grew up in "the projects," housing for low-income families. They were living in a mobile home when their only son, Mark, was born. Mark remembers always being unusually close to his mother (who "is good at taking care of people") but had mixed feelings about his father. Although Bill played ball with him and would help coach, Mark also often heard, "Get off my lap. . . . I'm trying to watch the game." When Bill left a dance floor with another woman but became angry when Andrea then had a male friend take her home, Andrea decided to separate from Bill. When Andrea told Mark of her decision to divorce, her son replied, "Now maybe you can find someone who will love you." Bill pressed for reconciliation: Sometimes he brought Andrea flowers and sometimes yelled obscenities at her for making him leave. On one occasion Bill brought Mark home from visitation and began to threaten

Andrea. Van, a divorced attorney whom Andrea eventually married, came from the next room and physically threw Bill out of the house as Andrea was attempting to remove Mark from the scene. Mark remembers feeling from this time that he had found someone who was willing to protect him and his mother. Van had two sons, one slightly older and one slightly younger than Mark. He married Andrea soon after the divorce, and they moved to an adjacent town. Mark had no trouble adjusting to the new school or neighborhood, one of a higher social class than where he had lived. The primary change was that he now played soccer as well as baseball.

After separation, Bill had moved in with his parents and brought his son for visitation every weekend. Mark liked the frequency but was bothered that his father was drinking a lot. He now realizes that both his father and paternal grandfather were alcoholics. Visitation decreased after the incident with Van, and when the marriage occurred Bill refused to pay child support and then "skipped." Bill called once or twice a year for the next few years, and then even this contact stopped. During this period Bill remarried and was divorced by a woman with whom Mark did not even talk on the phone. Mark continued to hear about his father at times and knew that he was in jail as a result of using both alcohol and hard drugs. Now, at the age of 20, Mark does not know where his biological father is, or even if he is alive. At times Mark felt some brief distress that he had a "loser" for a father. When Mark was 14, he was legally adopted by Van, whom he now considers his actual father. He thinks that because Van is such a good father, life has in some ways been simpler for him than for those people who continue interactions with a biological parent and a stepparent. He says this because of his observations of his stepsiblings. From the beginning he got along well with them, and they all welcomed the adoption in order to "feel complete as real brothers." However, they did move back and forth from one home to another. Further, there was not a good relationship between the stepsons and Andrea; Mark has been bothered by seeing his mother's pain at this.

Mark has always earned good grades and has behaved well at home and school. His mother often reminds him of the genetic history of alcoholism; he drinks seldom and cautiously. He has had no serious romantic relationships but thinks this is because he is both "picky" and still young. Although Mark has entered college, he doesn't have a career goal other than knowing that he would like to work with young people, if in no other way than informally as a coach.

One of the earliest studies to examine the relationship between step-parents and stepchildren (Bowerman & Irish, 1962) surveyed 25,000 seventh- through twelfth-graders from never-divorced or remarried families. Stepparents were rated lower than the biological parents, and stepmothers were rated lower than stepfathers. There were no comparisons with divorced parents. This finding was recently replicated (White et al., 1985). Sauer and Fine (1988) found that even young adult offspring rate relationships with stepmothers lower than with custodial biological mothers. In contrast, stepfathers were not rated differently than the fathers, presumably primarily noncustodial.

The problem that the stepmother faces has been interpreted as arising from the fact that she is more often the disciplinarian. It appears that in general she is more often the caretaker, also. Santrock, Sitterle, and Warshak (1988) found that stepmothers, as compared to stepfathers, were more likely to take their stepchildren to and from recreational activities, to discuss problems with their stepchildren, and to be perceived by the stepchildren as involved in discipline and school activities. Clinical observation and empirical research suggest that the older the child, the more difficulty there is in establishing a good stepparent-stepchild bond (Walker, Rogers, & Messinger, 1977). That is, adolescents, who are pushing for self-determination may particularly resent someone new in an authority position. An adolescent may also turn a younger sibling against the stepparent (Jones, 1978).

It is important, however, to remember that stepchildren generally are at least moderately close to their stepparents (Ganong & Coleman, 1987). Research describing the variables that influence these relationships is sorely needed. For example, stepparenting is more positive, especially for stepmothers, with live-in stepchildren than with those who live elsewhere (Crosbie-Burnett, 1991); joint custody is associated with better relationships with stepparents (Crosbie-Burnett, 1991); and the adult-child relationships are closer when families pool financial resources (Coleman & Ganong, 1989).

Research has also found gender differences in adaptation to remarriage of custodial mothers. A variety of studies has found that girls have more trouble accepting and interacting with stepfathers than do boys (e.g., Vuchinich, Hetherington, Vuchinich, & Clingempeel, 1991). Clingempeel, Brand, and Ievoli (1984) reported that girls, as compared to boys, report less love and more detachment toward stepmothers as well as toward stepfathers. They also exhibit more problem behavior and are less verbally positive.

Little is known about the relationship between stepsiblings. Ambert (1986) reported that the experience is more positive when the children are living in the same household rather than seeing one another as a result of visitation. Autobiographies of divorce suggest that stepsibling relationships vary perhaps even more than sibling relationships. Factors affecting stepsibling interactions could include differential treatment, limited time together, and uncertainties as to whether a remarriage will last.

A birth following remarriage results in a half-sibling. White et al. (1985) reported that younger half-siblings are associated with greater attachment in the present family, to both the original parent and the stepparent. However, Ambert (1986) found that the impact varies with the gender of the stepparent and whether the half-siblings live together.

A number of offspring experience not only a parental divorce and remarriage, but an additional marital disruption with one or both parents again divorcing. Peterson and Zill (1986) found that with a second maternal divorce, fewer than 1 in 10 children reported a positive relation with both parents. About three times as many have positive relations if the custodial mother never remarried, or if there is just one remarriage.

Relationships with Grandparents

The effects of divorce on grandparent-grandchild relationships have rarely been studied. However, the results of these studies suggest that fluctuations in family structure may influence grandparents' involvement with their grandchildren. Ahrons and Bowman (1982) interviewed grandmothers whose son or daughter had divorced to determine their views of the effect upon relationships with their grandchildren, their own children, and former in-laws. These women continued to provide support to their divorced child and did not view the divorce as having had a negative impact on their own lives. In a longitudinal study, Clingempeel, Colyar, Brand, and Hetherington (1992) repeatedly interviewed the offspring, their mothers and their maternal grandparents from divorced, non-divorced, and remarried families. Their data show that maternal grandparents, particularly grandfathers, were more involved with children in single-mother families than in non-divorced or remarried families. We might expect the perceptions and involvement of the parents of the noncustodial parent to be different. Unfortunately, no such data are available.

Overview

Predictably, some relationships are affected by the major changes that accompany parental divorce. The effects, however, are highly variable and depend upon gender, developmental stage, and the behavior of others. The variability of these effects is perhaps most dramatically illustrated in stepfamilies.

Although it is true that on the basis of mean differences, divorced fathers have less productive relationships with their children than do mothers, this results from interactions and behaviors that can also occur in married families.

In addition to being valued for itself, closeness to fathers has been linked to a number of positive outcomes for adolescent or young adult offspring. For example, LeCroy (1988) found that late adolescents had higher self-esteem and fewer behavior problems with greater father closeness. The degree of mother closeness did not predict either of these variables. Other research suggests that greater father closeness is related to less use of illicit drugs by females (Brook, Whiteman, Gordon, & Brook, 1984), higher social competence (Bell, Avery, Jenkins, Feld, & Schoenrock, 1985), higher self-trust or faith in one's ability to complete a task (Earl, 1987), and, for males, lack of shyness and comfort in same-sex peer relationships (Bell et al., 1985). Again, more research is needed to determine whether these associations also occur for divorced families.

Is it possible for parents who are not living together to socialize their children so that offspring do get a good education, learn how to find and maintain jobs, develop lifelong relationships, and deal with the inevitable stress and frustration of life while still enjoying living? In other words, is it possible for divorced adults to continue to parent? The data described here suggests that they can. Furthermore, offspring of divorced parents prefer their present family structure and environment to what had existed earlier (Neugebauer, 1989).

Summary

- Differences in the mental health and parenting behaviors of divorced and non-divorced parents may result from the stress of the divorce process, or it may be that those with problems are more likely to divorce.
- Both male and female adults are potentially capable of parenting.
- There is little evidence to support the convention that mothers be preferred as custodial parents.
- Although there are political reasons for preferring joint custody to other arrangements, the empirical evidence suggests that custody decisions should be based on other factors.
- Visitation with a caring, responsive, noncustodial parent can enhance the functioning of children. However, interaction with noncustodial parents often decreases over time, and there are conditions under which the relationship with the noncustodial parent can be harmful.

- Generally, offspring feel less close to noncustodial parents than to custodial parents and less close to fathers than to mothers, although there is considerable variation between offspring.
- Decreased feelings of closeness to noncustodial fathers are the result of specific behaviors that may be more likely among divorced fathers than never-divorced fathers rather than a result of the divorce per se.
- Relationships among members of stepfamilies can be strained, particularly when adolescents are involved.

5

Cognitive Performance and School Achievement

Preview

Psychologists distinguish between cognitive and affective variables. Cognition includes thought, beliefs, and information processing, whereas affect includes feelings and emotions. Our ability to process information and to remember things can be adversely affected by a highly upset emotional state. The ideas and beliefs that we hold may upset us emotionally. Although it is not possible to separate cognitive and affective processes completely, this chapter focuses on possible effects of divorce upon offsprings' cognitive development, especially in the realm of schooling.

Performance in School

The empirical research concerning the relation between single mothering and school performance has been reviewed many times. As in the other areas we consider, this research is often not specific to divorce, and groups studied include a variety of forms of "father absence." As a further complication, narrative reviews of this literature have reached varying conclusions. Herzog and Sudia (1973) examined the research published prior to 1968 and concluded that findings were too inconsistent to support any generalizations. Five years later, Shinn (1978) concluded that father absence was often associated with poor performance on cognitive tests. A few years after that, Hetherington, Cox, and Cox (1981) found no clear link between depressed test scores and growing up in a one-parent household. Not long after, Hetherington, Camara, and Featherman (1983) concluded that there were small effects that were mediated by a variety of factors.

Two meta-analyses provide some clarification. One meta-analysis (Salzman, 1987) of 137 studies published through 1986 reviewed research using intelligence tests, scholastic aptitude tests, achievement tests, and school grades, and considered the amount of difference between single-mother and two-parent groups. The "average" child living with two parents scored higher than 59 percent of the offspring of single mothers. A second meta-analysis (Amato & Keith, 1991a) also reported that the academic achievement of children of divorce was lower than that of children in two-parent families ($d = -.16$). This is *not* a large difference and is likely to be an overestimate of the effect because methodologically more sophisticated studies produced smaller effect sizes. Further, this review considered only published studies, which are likely to report larger effects than studies that are not published.

Standardized Tests

Standardized tests are frequently considered superior to grades as a measure of cognitive capabilities. The tests are more objective and can be directly compared across schools, and a school grade results from a single individual's judgment. Even though standardized measures have shown generally high reliability and validity, making them good predictors of academic success for the general population of school children, the extent to which they predict the performance of specific groups, such as offspring of divorce, is largely unknown. Furthermore, although scores on such tests are generally stable over time, they are known to fluctuate during times of stress in the lives of those being tested. Researchers rarely report the timing of the divorce in relation to when the tests were given, and relevant longitudinal data do not exist. One possible result is that small differences that may be found between offspring of divorce and other offspring could be attributed to stress and be expected to subside in time (Hetherington et al., 1983).

On standardized tests of intelligence, Salzman's meta-analysis (1987) found that the average difference between offspring in one- and two-parent families is only about 4 IQ points. This difference is small and would not be apparent to the casual observer (Cohen, 1977). Furthermore, random samples of children from divorced and non-divorced families are likely to differ on intelligence test scores unless the groups are equated for parental education or parental intelligence; the lower social classes are somewhat more likely to divorce, and these groups are known to differ in average ability.

In a more sophisticated study, Ricciuti and Scarr (1990) investigated biological and family risk factors for cognitive functioning of 2-year-old children in Bermuda. Using the Bailey Scale of Mental Development, the study showed that children whose fathers were not living with them had lower scores, particularly when the children also had low birth weight. The authors argued that low-birth-weight status in a single-mother home was exacerbated by and contributed to the instability of the environment. That is, the infants were both influenced by and contributing to the stress and instability of their own environment.

On standardized achievement tests, the meta-analysis (Salzman, 1987) found that the average child from a divorced family was 3 to 7 months behind the average child of married parents. This meta-analysis did not consider mediating factors that have been found by individual studies to be influential, but instead considered average group differences. More recent studies not included in that meta-analysis have been inconsistent. Several studies (Beer, 1989; Hawkins & Eggebeen, 1991; Hofmann & Zipco, 1986; Vandamme & Schwartz, 1985) have not found consistent differences between groups, whereas other studies have found lower scores for children from both divorced and remarried families (Boyd & Parish, 1985) and for adolescents of divorced parents in an African sample (Cherian, 1989). Kinard and Reinherz (1986) found that only those from recently divorced families scored lower than those from married families; this study did control for social class. Kaye (1988–89), in contrast, found that over a five-year period, the offspring of divorce fell further behind those in non-divorced families. Such inconsistencies are to be expected when differences are small and when they are influenced by other factors related to parental divorce.

Some have predicted that children in homes without fathers would also have a different pattern of ability for mathematical as compared to verbal skills. Traditional ideas about sex typing suggest that boys should score higher on tests of mathematical skills than on verbal skills, and that the reverse should be the pattern for girls. It follows from this line of reasoning that boys without adult male models should exhibit the female pattern, but the data have not confirmed this empirically (Hetherington et al., 1983).

Taken together, these data suggest that the difference in intelligence and achievement test scores between offspring in one- and two-parent families is small and largely attributable to aspects of social class and to stress and instability of the environment. Accordingly, it is unlikely that the differences represent true differences in ability.

School Grades

School grades reflect the ability to adapt to the expectations of teachers and to the system and should be considered an index of scholastic adjustment (Hetherington et al., 1983). Salzman's meta-analysis (1987) found that school grades were related to parental divorce to about the same extent as were standardized achievement tests. Several more recent studies have continued to find lower grade point averages for children of divorce as compared to those in non-divorced homes (Beer, 1989; Boyd & Parish, 1985; Hetherington et al., 1983; Kaye, 1988–89; Wentzel, 1991). These findings might result from all children doing somewhat less well following divorce. It is more likely that lower group averages result from some children who are not affected and from others who are noticeably affected. Such an effect could be temporary or longer-lasting.

Estimates of the percentage of children of divorce who do not achieve their academic potential vary. Wallerstein (1987) reported that about 40 percent in her sample of children of divorce were "under-achieving" at the ten-year follow-up. Bisnaire, Firestone, and Rynard (1990) found that 30 percent of their sample experienced marked decreases in academic performance following parental separation, and that the decrease was still evident three years later. McLoughlin and Whitfield (1984) indicated that only 12 percent of the adolescents in their sample believed that their school performance had deteriorated. Children may not be aware of the changes in their performance, or they may prefer not to acknowledge difficulties.

In this as in other instances, differences may result from a variety of factors associated with but not inherent in divorce. One argument is that the findings are not due to real differences in intellectual ability. Lower achievement ratings by teachers may result from the perception that these children lack interest or motivation to learn in the school setting (Hetherington et al., 1983). They are then less likely to be perceived as the prototypical "good" students and end up with lower grades. As discussed in Chapter 2, teachers expect children of divorce to perform less well on school-related dimensions (Ball, Newman, & Scheuren, 1984; Guttman & Broudo, 1989; Guttman, Geva, & Gefen, 1988; Santrock & Tracy, 1978). Teachers' expectations are determined by attributes considered most desirable by educated members of the middle class, and one of these characteristics is that a child's parents live together rather than being divorced (Rist, 1970).

Alternatively, differences in school grades may result from factors related to family functioning rather than to divorce or to single parenting. For example, two studies have reached different conclusions about the importance of access to both parents. One (Bisnaire, Firestone, & Rynard, 1990) found that access to both parents was associated with better academic achievement, whereas the other (Furstenberg, Morgan, & Allison, 1987) found that paternal contact was not related to school achievement. The second study was a national probability sample with children from a wide range of socioeconomic classes, where many of the children had no contact at all with their fathers. It is possible that, within a sample of middle class families and responsible fathers, the amount of contact would make a difference.

Family conflict is another frequently considered variable. Grade point averages were negatively affected by parental conflict in two studies (Long, Forehand, Fauber, & Brody, 1987; McCombs & Forehand, 1989). In the first, marital status per se was not associated with school achievement. McCombs and Forehand also found that conflict between the child and the custodial mother was related to school grades, with less intense levels of conflict for those who had higher grade averages. Because this is a correlational finding, the low grades could have preceded the conflict. It may be important, too, that the data were gathered from the adolescents themselves rather than from the parents.

In summary, the evidence concerning the impact of parental divorce on classroom performance suggests that on the average, offspring of divorce do receive lower grades than offspring of never-divorced families. Clearly, this difference is small, and family stress does influence school performance.

School Behavior

Some school behaviors, like absences and tardiness, may be studied by collecting data from records in the permanent files. However, most information about behavior in school has been gathered by means of ratings most often made by teachers. Parents have occasionally been used, but children have rarely been asked for their own perceptions.

One reason for including data from all of these sources is that they may yield different results. One study (Kinard & Reinherz, 1986) found that teachers rated offspring of divorce as having problems with productivity, whereas the parents of these children did not. A large-scale probability sample (Allison & Furstenberg, 1989) provided information at two points in time for children in families with marital dissolution. Teachers reported that children of divorced as compared to married families had more problems in 1976 but not in 1981. Parents reported more academic difficulty on both occasions; children's self-reports at both times were that they were not having more academic difficulties. Parent and teacher ratings are perhaps more likely than those of the children to be influenced by expectations. Although children may on some occasions be better reporters of what is happening with them, that may not be the case regarding overt behaviors. It is difficult to determine the extent to which teachers' perceptions of conduct problems and study patterns are accurate. Obviously, however, this is the data that is primarily available in studies dealing with specific behaviors that may relate to problems in school.

As a result of their review of the literature, Hetherington et al. (1983) concluded that offspring of single parents are tardy and absent from school more often than those from two-parent homes. Vandamme and Schwartz (1985) found their Australian single-parent sample to have higher absentee rates as well.

Guidubaldi and Perry (1985) compared divorced-family and married-family children; after controlling statistically for IQ, they found that divorced-family girls showed more inattention in the classroom, exhibited more irrelevant talk, and were more intellectually dependent. Divorced-family boys were rated lower on work effort. Statistical controls for family income reduced some of these differences.

Recent research (Woodman & Lewis, 1990) confirmed that children of divorce overall showed more immature behavior in early elementary school than did those in non-divorced families. However, regression analysis found that it was not marital status that predicted problem behaviors but rather the parental relationship, measured by such things as quality and frequency of interaction between the parents.

As with other areas, the differences between samples of children from divorced or married homes yield fairly consistent but small differences in school behaviors. These differences can be put in perspective by noting that they are probably smaller than the differences found between boys and girls (e.g., Allison & Furstenberg, 1989).

Perceptions of Competence and Achievement Motivation

Research findings comparing offsprings' perceptions of their competence or their achievement motivation are scarce and contradictory. One study (Long, Forehand, Fauber, & Brody, 1987) found that actual school competence was not related to whether parents were divorced but rather was associated with amount of reported parental conflict. However, the adolescents' self-perceived levels of competence were related to parental marital status, with those from divorced families perceiving themselves as less competent. In contrast, McLoughlin and Whitfield (1984) interviewed a non-representative sample of Caucasian adolescents whose divorcing parents were in conflict over child custody. The vast majority said that their school performance had either improved or not been affected by the divorce.

Contrary to their expectations, Vandamme and Schwartz (1985) reported higher achievement motivation scores among elementary school children whose parents divorced than those whose parents were married. However, in college students, Greenfeld and Teevan (1986) reported more fear of failure among students from divorced homes than those from non-divorced, two-parent homes. Interestingly, fear of failure scores were highest for those whose fathers were deceased. Fry and Scher (1984) reported decreases over a five-year period in achievement motivation for 10-year-old sons of divorced parents, but not for daughters when compared to offspring in non-divorced families.

■ _____

Life Story

Della

Della, a 22-year-old college senior, grew up in Wisconsin. Her parents, Tom and Barbara, married when they were 20 and had just completed two years of college. It is open family history that Barbara was pregnant with Della and that both families were pressuring them to marry. Tom went to work as a salesman and Barbara became a housewife. Additional children, Bob and Bill, were born three and five years later. Della does not remember ever feeling that her parents were happy together, although there was little overt conflict. She does vividly remember one incident. At a gathering of Tom's family, Tom and a number of other adults became intoxicated and began to use profanity; when nearby children were asked to carry beer or to mix drinks, Barbara decided to remove her children and asked Tom to leave also. (In retrospect, Della realizes that a number of Tom's relatives, including his father, are alcoholics and that her father also has had a drinking problem.) He refused, and Barbara left with the children. Tom, who believes in traditional gender roles in which men make decisions for the family, was outraged that Barbara had gone against his wishes. Not long after, when Della was 9, her mother decided on divorce, which her father opposed. Tom briefly threatened to ask for custody, and during that time bought many things for the children and took them on expensive outings. Barbara was granted full custody of the children, and Tom was allowed open visitation. Barbara began to work full time at a job that required her to commute for a considerable distance. Della not only had to help with housework but also supervise her younger brothers after school and during the day in the summer. At the time she hated not being able to play with her friends, as she previously had done, but in retrospect she believes that it helped her to become a more independent and responsible person.

Della liked the arrangement wherein she was allowed to choose when she would visit her father, as it made it seem that they were more like the usual family. The time they spent together gradually decreased, in part because Tom was spending more time at work, and successfully increasing his income, and also because he was actively involved in town politics. He was eventually elected mayor. For the past 8 years, Tom has lived with a woman who has a daughter about Della's age. They have no plans to marry. Barbara has never remarried or lived with anyone.

Della's father was ordered to pay both child support and alimony for a few years. Della believes that he would sometimes send payments late in order to annoy Barbara. Although he is clearly financially well off, Tom has resisted supporting either Della or her brothers for extras such as school trips, athletic camps, or even college. Della has obtained about one tenth of her college expenses from her father, who was not legally required to support her after the age of 18. Bob and Bill are working for athletic scholarships. Della wishes that her family could have gone to counseling in order to help them deal with issues. As she was growing up, Della often discussed her concerns with a best friend whose parents had been multiply married and divorced. They tried to understand what made a healthy relationship. Della does not recall ever crying or feeling sad about her parents' split; she does remember anger at what she saw as her father's selfishness regarding his children. A high achiever both in school and other activities, Della has been angry because nothing she ever did seemed good enough for her father's interest or attention. Similarly, Tom will not take his athletic sons to games; they bore him. In contrast, Della's mother continuously put her children's needs before her own. While she is away at college, Della still talks with her mother twice a week. She has polite visits with her father both when she returns home and when he comes once a year for "Dad's Day."

Della is applying for graduate school and plans to complete a doctorate. Although she has had several committed relationships of over a year, Della is unsure about marriage. She sometimes wonders if it is really possible to "have it all," as she would like to do.

Overall, Della feels that the divorce was not only the best thing for her parents, especially for her mother, Della's model of a competent and caring person, but also that she herself has become more mature and wise because she has successfully learned how to deal with these experiences.

High School Dropout and College Attendance Rates

One of the consistent findings in the literature is that children from single-mother families complete fewer years of school. A meta-analysis (Amato & Keith, 1991b) of 18 studies showed that adults who experienced parental divorce as children obtained less education than offspring whose parents had not divorced. Even when controlling for race and socioeconomic class, these children are more likely to drop out of high school than are children from two-parent families (Carlson, 1979; Keith & Finlay, 1988; Krein & Beller, 1988; McLanahan, 1985; McLanahan & Booth, 1989; McLanahan & Bumpass, 1988; Shaw, 1982). Moreover, the longer a child spends in a single-parent family, the less time she or he will spend in school (Haurin, 1992; Krein & Beller, 1988).

One possibility is that children in single-mother homes are dropping out of school because they are doing less well, although considering the slight achievement difference discussed earlier, this is unlikely. Hetherington et al. (1983) suggested two other factors. Offspring may be dropping out because of early pregnancies and marriage, or they may be terminating their schooling because of economic necessity and early entrance into the labor force. In one study, maternal income accounted for about 40 percent to 50 percent of the difference in high school dropout rates of children from single-mother and two-parent families, but the differences persisted even after income was controlled statistically (McLanahan & Booth, 1989).

McLanahan (1985) conducted a large-scale study investigating the relations between family structure, poverty, and whether the respondent was in school at age 17 or had graduated from high school. Single parenting decreased the probability of being in school by about 5 percent for Caucasians and about 13 percent for African Americans. These percentages were reduced when some demographic variables, including parental level of education, were controlled. McLanahan investigated economic deprivation as an explanation for the probability of remaining in school. Among the families she studied, a $10,000 change in income altered the probability of being in school by 17 percent for Caucasians and about 13 percent for African Americans. Having a family on welfare reduced the probability of being in school by 35 percent for Caucasians, but not for African Americans. Neither maternal employment nor adolescent employment explained why adolescents in single-parent families were less likely to be in school than those in two-parent households. Effects were not consistent for all categories of single-parent families. For Caucasians, those living with separated but not yet divorced mothers were worse off than all other groups. The effects of recent marital disruption were dramatic but were no longer significant after five years of being in a single-parent family.

Less is known about the effects of parental divorce upon offsprings' college graduation. Wallerstein (1987) noted that many of the young adults in her study were "drifting," not in school, and obtaining less education than one would expect, judging by their parents' achievements. In addition, offspring of divorce may not obtain financial support for college, even from fathers who can afford it (Wallerstein & Corbin, 1986).

In summary, parental divorce may affect the offspring's level of education if there is a resultant major economic problem. Stress associated with recent separation seems to play some role as well. There may be other factors that are influential in some particular cases.

Life Story

Jon

Jon, now 25, has supported himself since 16. He married at 19 and is now working to enable both himself and his wife to attend college full-time. They have one 5-year-old daughter. The younger of two children of B. J. and Shirley, Jon lived in Texas until the time of his parents' divorce. Prior to the separation, Jon's parents had fought for years, often over minor matters such as why B. J. had come to the table 3 minutes late.

Dishes were thrown by both parents. In the most intense fight, viewed by Jon, his mother pointed a gun at his father. Perhaps more disturbing, Shirley would lock herself in the bathroom with a gun and pretend to shoot herself, although actually shooting the gun out the window. Jon was greatly affected by these scenes, crying or going to his room. Toward his mother, Jon harbors resentment that does not lessen with time.

Jon was 9 when the separation and divorce occurred. His brother, David, who was five years older, asked to live with B. J. Jon suspects that David did not wish to be a baby-sitter for a younger brother. Because B. J. couldn't keep a child and travel for his work, David then went to live with other relatives, never returning to live with Shirley. With a few hours' notice, Jon was moved by his mother from a school where he had been class president to live in another state. First they moved into a motel, and Jon was kept out of school by his mother for months until they moved to a trailer, where they lived for years. Jon remembers frequently waking up in the middle of the night with roaches crawling on him. Shirley had not previously worked and had no marketable skills, so money was short. She also went to a nearby bar, sometimes being gone for several days and leaving Jon alone. At other times she would bring men home to spend the night, and Jon could hear them having sex in the adjacent room.

Even after Shirley became employed, Jon usually went to bed hungry and cried himself to sleep, not just because of the hunger. "The crying then turned into hatred toward my parents and anybody around me. I remember getting into a lot of fights. However, my grades actually improved. The only thing that I cared about was school. . . . This was the only way I could cope with everything." He does believe that counseling would have helped. Jon had begun reading the Bible when he was young, and was helped by prayer. Religion is important to him still, and he attends church as often as possible. He believes that if his parents had been more religious, the divorce would not have been as bad, or perhaps not even occurred. Still, he believes that God has a purpose for each of us and that things happen to us for a reason.

B. J. sent support but no extra money. Jon saw his father only at Christmas until the age of 13, when he began to spend entire summers with him. These were usually pleasant, except that Jon was annoyed with his father's lies about dating. When Jon left home after high school, he and his mother quarreled, and they did not speak for five years. Jon asked both parents for assistance in paying for college. His father refused, and his mother was herself in debt. For several years Jon and his father did not speak. Currently, B. J. calls Jon about once a week. Jon talks with Shirley every few weeks when she calls.

Jon's parents have not seen one another since the divorce. Neither has remarried, although B. J. is now talking about a romantic relationship. Each continues to complain to David about the other. At most, Jon has seen his brother, David, five times since the divorce. David, who abuses both alcohol and drugs, dropped out of school in the ninth grade and is currently in prison.

Jon is earning a degree in writing. He believes that life will be a failure unless he has a successful career. Recently, Jon and his wife have had problems. She, too, experienced parental divorce, and they both are determined to work things out so that their daughter does not have to endure a divorce. Even so, Jon knows that his parents would have continued fighting if they had remained together. He vows that he will never fight in front of his daughter and say the kinds of things that he heard from his parents.

Mediating Variables

As in other areas of research, the apparent effects upon cognitive and school performance are not due directly to parental divorce but to other mediating factors. We can conclude that the effects of single mothering upon school achievement and behavior are similar for both sexes (McLanahan, 1985; Salzman, 1987). Although Salzman (1987) concluded that race and socioeconomic status have little effect, a large-scale study of 6- to 11-year-old children showed that group mean differences disappear when socioeconomic status was controlled (Svanum, Bringle, & McLaughlin, 1982). Salzman (1987) also considered age in her meta-analysis and found that effects are greater in elementary and junior high school than for preschool or college. However, these are cross-sectional data with different kinds of measures used with different age groups, so drawing conclusions would be premature.

Stress comes in a variety of forms, and high levels of stress and anxiety interfere with cognitive efficiency. Any behavior adversely affected by stress is likely to change when parents separate and at times of high parental conflict. Finding lower achievement scores only for those with recent family disruption (Kinard & Reinherz, 1986) supports this interpretation.

Academic performance may also be affected when children change schools, as often happens following divorce. We do not have data on the general effect of school change, but for many this is likely to be a difficulty. Harvey (1991) has reported that "new kids," particularly boys, are more often referred to school psychologists.

Some research has shown that children in stepfamilies score similarly to children in married families (Boyd & Parish, 1985). Although a remarriage may reduce economic worries, in certain circumstances the presence of a stepparent may actually cause more stress. However, there is no systematic study of this variable, so no conclusions can be made.

Negative effects apparently associated with parental divorce may also result from the child's interaction with the individual parents, or from conflict within the family. McCombs and Forehand (1989) reported that among adolescents living with recently divorced mothers, offspring with higher grade point averages had mothers who were less depressed, better educated, and who experienced less conflict with ex-spouses and with their children. In addition, Forehand, Wierson, Thomas, Armistead, Kempton, and Fauber (1990) showed that high conflict between the parents and low visitation with the noncustodial father was detrimental to cognitive functioning.

In addition to stress-related factors, parental expectations can also influence academic achievement. Barker (B. Barker, personal communication, 1991) found that divorced mothers had lowered expectations for children's math achievement. These children were matched with others for original achievement level and were later found to be doing less well.

Parents also have an impact through the opportunities they provide. MacKinnon, Brody, and Stoneman (1986) evaluated the home environments of preschool children in divorced and non-divorced families. They found that children from divorced homes received less cognitive stimulation than children in non-divorced homes, and that this was particularly true for boys. "Boys from mother-headed, single-parent homes had fewer toys, games, and reading materials and a less rich physical environment than all other children" (p. 75). However, a similar study failed to find a difference attributable to single-mothering (Rosenthal, Leigh, & Elardo, 1985/1986).

Finally, children of divorce may also learn less effective strategies for achieving high test scores. Guttman, Amir, and Katz (1987) reported that these children withdraw from difficult testing situations earlier than was optimal. In this study, children of divorced families spent less time on the testing task, attempted fewer problems, and performed less well than children of non-divorced families. For a sample of Israeli boys, Guttman (1987) also reported that those with divorced parents had higher test-anxiety scores than those from non-divorced families.

Overview

Although there does appear to be a small difference between groups, the relation between single parenting and a child's academic achievement is complex. Hetherington et al. (1983) suggested the following:

> The need for single parents to rely on their children for assistance with household and child-care tasks and routines of daily living may result in less time available for these children to attend to achievement-related tasks. Children who are expected to assist with preparation of meals, care for younger siblings, and perhaps even find part-time jobs to assist with financial management of the household may be unable to concentrate their efforts on school work. This, in turn, may result in lower grades and less positive evaluations by teachers and school personnel. (p. 271)

Given the available data, we cannot conclude that parental divorce causes anything with respect to intellectual ability or school performance. However, it can be viewed as a marker for other variables that can have direct effects. These include such things as social class, parental conflict, or lack of supervision. The economic and emotional stress that can accompany parental divorce contributes to or exacerbates the small differences in cognitive performance and school achievement between offspring of divorced and non-divorced parents. In other words, although parental divorce is related to school performance, changes in school performance are not the inevitable result of parental divorce. Longitudinal data beginning before the divorce and following students over several years would be invaluable to our understanding of the dynamics of these processes.

Because of the long-term consequences, the most distressing of these findings is that offspring of divorce complete fewer years of school. Lower levels of education are associated with poverty. We will see that educational attainment is also related to the likelihood of divorce. Thus, a divorced custodial mother who lives in poverty is more likely to have children who continue to live in poverty and perhaps who experience their own divorce.

Summary

- Offspring of divorce receive lower scores on standardized tests and lower school grades when compared to offspring from non-divorced families.
- Offspring of divorce may behave less like the model student than do offspring of non-divorced parents.
- Offspring of divorce complete fewer years of schooling than offspring from non-divorced families.
- These differences are small and are likely to be the result of factors such as economic problems and emotional stress.

6

Gender Roles

Preview

For some time many have believed that appropriate sex typing is a good indicator of psychological adjustment. People are sex typed to the extent that they have incorporated characteristics that are considered appropriate to their biological sex. Characteristics about which we develop ideas of sex appropriateness include such qualities as physical appearance and movement, behaviors, personality traits, and occupations. The normative notions that a society develops for the sexes have been referred to as sex roles or gender roles. (The early literature in this field referred to sex roles, perhaps implying that these roles were based on biological sex differences. Recently, many prefer the term *gender* roles, to emphasize that these are most often arbitrarily chosen standards.) In this chapter we consider the predictions that theories of gender-role development make for offspring of single mothers. We also review the empirical evidence on the relation between single parenting and sex-typed behavior of offspring.

Theoretical Predictions for Offspring of Divorce

Four major theoretical perspectives have influenced the study of gender roles and made predictions for children whose fathers do not live with them, as is often the case when parents divorce. Psychoanalytic models of sex typing suggest that sex-appropriate behavior results from identification with the same-sex parent. Social learning models focus on the differential administration of rewards and punishments. Cognitive-developmental models highlight the child's active thinking and cognitive maturity. Information-processing models also emphasize the child's active thinking, but do not emphasize developmental processes as the source of schemas or as the means of changing them (Huston, 1983).

Psychoanalytic Models

Freudian identification theory (Freud, 1949; 1950) suggests that parents play a primary role in the development of the appropriate gender role. In the absence of the father, as was assumed in the case of divorce, the son has no salient male model with whom to identify and no major rival for his mother's affections. As a result, the theory predicts that the mother-son relationship may become oversexualized (Neubauer, 1960). This incestuous reality becomes a source of great guilt to the young boy. Unable to transfer his desire from his mother to other females, he is expected to reject females as love objects altogether. In addition, in the absence of the father and with no apparent reason to identify with another adult male, the boy's pre-Oedipal identification with the mother may persist so much that he may model his behavior after that of his mother. According to this theory, such modeling would hinder the boy's development of a masculine gender-role identity.

Much less emphasis has been placed on the role of the father in a daughter's Oedipal development. When the father is discussed by those who hold a psychoanalytic viewpoint, he is often described as having only indirect influence on the daughter by affecting the mother's relationship with the girl. Still, it is clear that Freud assumed that the daughter's shift of love-object choice hinged on the father's active participation in the family. Leonard (1966) described two possible outcomes for "father-absent" daughters. In the first, the girl provides herself with a fantasized relationship that includes an idealized image of her father. In an attempt to secure attention from both parents (even though the father is absent and may not be in contact with her), the girl may identify with the fantasy father and remain fixated at the boylike phase in development. In this way, the girl "retains her mother's love by being a father whom mother loves; and by becoming the boy that father was or wished for, is loved by him as well" (p. 329). In adolescence the girl may seek as love-object someone who fits her idealized image. In the second outcome, unable to give love, "the girl seeks a man who will 'father' her, or she uses her awareness of being attractive to boys to fulfill her need for satisfaction. Sexuality serves as a means to that end" (p. 333).

Other identification theories exist (e.g., Mowrer, 1950; Lynn, 1974), but none has been as influential as Freud's. Although the mechanisms are somewhat different and the effects differ in magnitude, identification theories predict that offspring of single mothers, particularly sons, will have difficulty in developing societally approved gender-role behaviors.

Social Learning Models

Social learning models (Mischel, 1966, 1970; Mussen, 1969) focus directly on the acquisition of sex-typed behaviors rather than on the process of "identification." According to these systems, the child must first learn to discriminate between sex-typed behavior patterns, then generalize from these specific learning experiences to new situations, and finally perform sex-typed behaviors. Sex-typed behaviors are thought to be acquired through the same learning principles as is any other aspect of behavior. Learning mechanisms include differential rewards and punishments, generalization, verbal mediation, modeling, and observation.

Social learning theorists suggest that children imitate the most salient model available. Due to the importance given to the same-sex parent as a model and a rewarder, one might predict that father absence would be deleterious to sons' gender-role development but not particularly harmful to that of daughters. Mischel (1970) suggested that father-absent children may be less adequately socialized in non-sex-typed behaviors as well.

Social learning theory also predicts that younger children may be more affected by the absence of the father than older children are. The assumption is that the father is a more salient model for the younger child. Peers and others outside the home seem to be more influential in later childhood, so father absence may be less detrimental then.

Finally, social learning theorists (Bandura & Walters, 1963) have suggested that due to changes in present-day culture (e.g., television) perhaps parents are less influential as models than they once were. If this is the case, father absence may be less detrimental to the development of children now than it was earlier.

Cognitive-Developmental Models

In 1966, Lawrence Kohlberg proposed a cognitive-developmental theory of gender-role development. He suggested that sex typing is a function of the child's active structuring of his or her own experience, rather than a passive product of rewards and punishments or of identification with an adult. He also suggested that gender-role concepts mature in the same way that other concepts develop.

According to Kohlberg, a child's gender-role identity is organized around gender identity (i.e., the child's self-categorization as a "boy" or "girl"). He suggested that this process of self-labeling begins with the child learning and hearing the verbal labels "boy" and "girl." The self-labeling process ends with a cognitive decision, "I am a girl." This produces a stable gender identity that is ultimately based on physical differences between the sexes. Once gender identity is established, children tend to value things related to their own sex, including the same-sex parent, because the child's cognitive processes are egocentric.

Because identification with the same-sex parent is a consequence of sex typing rather than a cause, it follows that father absence need not be deleterious to the gender-role development of either boys or girls. However, Kohlberg suggested that father absence may create a deleterious emotional climate that might retard the development of sex-typed characteristics.

Information-Processing/Schema Models

Information-processing or schema models de-emphasize identification and focus on how children come to be more or less sex typed through the development of gender-based schemas (Bem, 1979; Martin & Halverson, 1981). Schemas are cognitive structures that serve as theories to guide information processing. They allow people to structure their experience and to regulate their behavior, and also provide a basis for making inferences and interpretations.

These models make the basic assumption that children, as information processors, actively categorize information. In most cultures, gender is a stable dichotomy that allows for the organization and processing of large amounts of information. Once gender schemas have been established, the self-concept is assimilated into the gender schema. In this way, children learn which attributes are linked to their own sex and hence to themselves. Bem (1979, 1981) proposed that the schema acts as a standard or prototype against which children compare themselves; gender schemas then help to determine a child's self-worth. The male who is not athletic or the female who is not thin enough are likely to judge themselves as inadequate. In this way, the child is motivated to conform to cultural definitions of maleness or femaleness. From Bem's position, sex-typed individuals differ from others, not in how much masculinity or femininity they possess, but according to whether or not their self-concepts and behaviors are organized on the basis of gender.

The similarities between this approach and that of Kohlberg (1966) are numerous and obvious. However, the goal achieved by the cognitive structures is different. Kohlberg and other theorists appear to assume that "appropriate" sex typing is the most desired end state and a developmental goal. Schema theory implies that these cognitive structures are based in reality and are built as the result of the child's need to make sense out of his or her environment. If, for a particular child, gender-role categories were not so obvious or useful in information processing, then that child would not develop such schemas.

In the case of father-absent children, one might argue that their environment is less sex typed because the remaining parent will be forced to perform roles and exhibit qualities that she would not in a more traditional situation. That child would be less likely to develop well differentiated gender schemas, especially if this environmental difference occurred while the child was very young. However, when the child's world expands beyond the home (e.g., by attending school) gender is likely to become a more salient characteristic. The environment thus could give reason for gender schemas to develop. Gender schemas, then, are more directly the result of the salience of gender in the environment than of who is present or absent.

In sum, each theory described here predicts that father absence has the potential to affect sex typing. Most predict that father absence will have greater impact on boys than on girls, due to the presumed importance of the same-sex parent. As well, most predict that absence will more greatly affect a young child. However, each of the major theoretical perspectives emphasizes a different explanatory mechanism.

Most major theories assume that "appropriate" sex typing should be a goal for all children. That is, boys should be traditionally masculine: independent, aggressive, competitive, strong, and the like. In contrast, girls should be traditionally feminine: gentle and submissive, loving toward children, and nurturant. Obviously, definitions of desirable masculinity and femininity change over time. However, regardless of how much the definitions of masculinity and femininity change, the mechanisms responsible for their development should remain constant as long as boys and girls are expected to develop different characteristics.

Given the importance attributed to the same-sex parent, much of the literature addressing the effects of father absence and therefore, of single mothering on gender-role development in offspring, has focused on sons. The working hypothesis has stated that boys who lack a father also lack a traditionally sex-typed male role model or an appropriate object of identification, and are likely to experience difficulty developing a sex-typed gender-role identity. Many theorists (e.g., Freud, 1949; Mowrer, 1950; Parsons, 1955) have also suggested that adequate fathering is necessary for optimal gender-role development in daughters. Clinicians continue to use case reports to support an association between loss of father through divorce and a girl's resultant difficulty with feminine development (Lohr, Legg, Mendell, & Riemer, 1989).

Single Mothers and Gender-Role Development

In 1988, we published a comprehensive review of the literature on gender-role development in children reared by single mothers (Stevenson & Black, 1988). An additional literature search located only four similar studies (Boyd & Parish, 1984; Kagel & Schilling, 1985; Moran & Barclay, 1988; Serbin, Powlishta, & Gulko, 1993). These provided little new information.

Using meta-analytic techniques, we reviewed 67 studies that were conducted between 1946 and 1984. These studies produced 222 estimates of the magnitude of difference between offspring of single mothers and those living with both parents. Unfortunately for our current purpose, we had to include studies of single mothering for reasons other than divorce; few studies looked specifically at the consequences of parental divorce.

Negative effect size estimates indicate that offspring of single mothers were less sex stereotypical (e.g., boys scored lower on masculinity scales) than were offspring from two-parent families; positive estimates indicated the reverse. For males overall, the estimate of effect size was –.14 based on 116 effect-size estimates. Although small, this is a statistically significant difference. For females the mean effect size was –.02, based on 48 estimates. Clearly this was not statistically different from zero. Of the 222 estimates of effect size, 33 were clearly from samples of boys whose parents had divorced and 22 were from samples of girls whose parents had divorced. Mean estimates of effect size for these groups were not statistically significant for either sex.

Based on this latter finding, we might conclude that there is no effect of divorce on gender-role development in children. However, it is possible that mean effect-size estimates mask findings that may apply to more specific groups. For example, if young boys whose parents divorce are less masculine and older boys whose parents divorce are more masculine than their counterparts in non-divorced families, the overall mean would approximate zero.

To investigate this possibility, we used the larger study sample and considered a host of variables that could potentially mediate the relation between single mothering and various definitions of gender-role development. Some analyses considered characteristics of the offspring: the participant's race, socioeconomic status, age, and the context from which researchers had gained access to the sample of participants (e.g., schools; detention centers). We also determine if the findings depended on how gender-role development was measured as well as on other aspects of the research methodology. These analyses revealed that any overall conclusions should be qualified in a variety of ways.

Age of the Child

Many theories have emphasized the importance of the child's developmental status when considering the effects of divorce. According to the meta-analysis, preschool-aged boys are the most affected. However, interpretation of this result is difficult for two reasons. First, different types of measures are used with different age groups of children. Measures commonly used with young children—those that produced some of the largest effects—require children to choose between stereotypical toys and activities. Responses are scored as either masculine or feminine and are based on the assumption that masculinity and femininity are opposite ends of a continuum. These measures may overestimate the extent to which children are sex-stereotyped. Based on these measures, sons living with both parents were more likely than sons living with their mothers to choose masculine toys and activities for themselves or for another child whose sex was not specified. Observations of naturally occurring toy choices also show that children from single-mother families are somewhat more likely to play with other-sex and neutral toys (Brenes, Eisenberg, & Helmstadter, 1985).

Several factors may explain why young single-mothered boys make fewer stereotypical choices on measures of sex typing when compared to boys living with both parents. Although the effect could result from the absence of an appropriate male model, this variable may be irrelevant (Huston, 1983). Single-parent homes are somewhat less stereotypical than two-parent homes (MacKinnon, Brody, & Stoneman, 1982). It is unclear, however, whether this is because single mothers are less stereotypical than mothers in intact families (Kurdek & Siesky, 1980), because children in single-parent families develop different ideas about how boys and girls are to behave (Bem, 1981; Martin & Halverson, 1981) and have less knowledge of sex-typed activities and occupations (Serbin, Powlishta, & Gulko, 1993), because fathers more often enforce stereotypical roles in their children than mothers, or because of differences in child-rearing practices (Stevenson, 1988).

Measures used with older as compared to younger children show much smaller effects. Whether this is due to age or to a difference in the construct being measured is difficult to determine. An interesting exception to this generalization derives from data on sex typing of vocational choice. Two studies of college men showed that those who have experienced single mothering were less sex-stereotyped than those who had not. However, a large-scale study of men in female-concentrated occupations failed to find a relation between working in a female-dominated occupation and father absence of any variety (Hayes, 1989).

A second problem with interpreting the apparent finding that there is an effect from single mothering only at a particular young age deals with research design. These analyses were based on age at the time of the study, rather than on age at onset of single mothering. Therefore, age at onset and duration are confounded. Furthermore, several variables were confounded in the available studies. Without ample longitudinal data, not presently available, it is impossible to assess whether differences in attributes of the two groups are due to the developmental status of the child, the instability of the immediate situation, the lack of time to adjust to a new set of environmental demands, or some combination of these.

Race and Social Class

In our culture, social class and race are clearly related. In fact, the relation between these variables is so strong that it is sometimes appropriate to attribute race differences to social class. The meta-analysis showed that the effects were larger in the middle class than in the lower class and larger in African Americans than in Caucasians. Explaining these differences is difficult due to the confounding of variables. In comparison to Caucasians, African Americans not only experience a greater likelihood of divorce, but wait longer when marital problems arise before getting a divorce. In addition, they experience longer periods of being single between marriages (Kitson & Raschke, 1981; Norton & Glick, 1976). Under these circumstances, single-parent sons in African-American families may experience greater periods of instability and conflict and live in single-mother households for greater periods of time than Caucasian children. Unfortunately, we were unable to locate a single study that included middle-class African Americans. Our findings did show that the estimate of effect for lower-class Caucasians was not significant. The estimate for lower-class African Americans was more than twice that of middle-class Caucasians. This seems to indicate that these differences may be better explained by other correlates. Clearly, further investigation is necessary prior to conclusions about divorce and gender-role development in samples differing in race or social class.

Measurement Variables

Studies were rated as to their quality for our meta-analysis. The best-controlled studies were unique in that they dealt either with the duration of the absence or the presence of surrogate models. The best-quality studies produced nonsignificant estimates of effect size. Unpublished studies (mainly dissertations) have found less difference than those that have been published. These data suggest that those reviewers who do not consider unpublished studies are likely to expect the effects of single mothering to be larger than the overall evidence would support.

Reviews that rely heavily on case studies or on other nonrepresentative samples may also be biased. The meta-analysis showed that larger effect sizes were obtained from studies employing clinical samples than from studies of samples from schools or communities. As discussed earlier, studies of atypical groups can provide valuable information about the potential effects of divorce but should not be used as the basis for broad generalizations.

Cause of the absence analyses showed that boys whose fathers were absent due to military service were significantly more affected than other boys, while no evidence suggested that a father's death had an effect on gender-role development in boys. This again demonstrates the inadvisability of generalizing from one type of father absence to other types.

There was a discrepancy between behavior ratings, most often parent or teacher ratings, and self-report measures. The meta-analysis showed that on ratings of behaviors, sons of single mothers were more stereotypical than sons living with both parents; self-report measures found the opposite to be true. These results primarily occurred because the sons of single mothers were rated by others as more aggressive than were sons living with both parents. (Previous rating scales have often considered aggressive behavior to be an indication of strong masculinity.) Obviously, there are other possible explanations. The results may reflect an expectation that the raters hold for single-mothered boys rather than be accurate reflections of the boys' behavior. For example, teachers expect children of divorce to have more problems than children from non-divorced families (Santrock & Tracy, 1978; Levine, 1981). Perhaps, however, the observers were correct. We have already reported that many children of divorced parents have witnessed more conflict than other children; maybe sons of divorced parents express more overt aggression because they model their parents' behavior. Others (Block, Block, & Gjerde, 1986; Emery, 1982) have also shown that parental discord is more likely to affect boys than girls. Therefore, we should not be surprised to find boys behaving more aggressively in an emotionally frustrating situation. Maybe this aggressive behavior would be exhibited without an aggressive male model; some or many of these children are sufficiently upset to exhibit behavioral control problems.

These findings demonstrate the importance of knowing how gender roles are conceptualized. Also important is our finding that, on measures of masculinity and femininity when the constructs were conceptualized as two separate and independent characteristics, one- and two-parent boys did not differ. However, when masculinity and femininity were conceptualized as opposite ends of a single continuum, sons of single mothers were shown to be less stereotypical than sons living with both parents. Being less stereotypical does not mean that they were unmasculine and can be interpreted as beneficial to the child.

Certainly future research should consider the possibility that family structure influences different aspects of gender role in different ways (Biller, 1974).

Role Models of the Other Gender

Given the widespread belief that children need same-sex role models to be well-adjusted, single parents sometimes wonder whether they should find such role models for their children when the same-sex parent does not reside in the home. Apparently, this is the assumption behind programs such as Big Brothers or Big Sisters as well as behind policies that encourage more men to become elementary school teachers and child-care workers.

Indeed, based on the theories discussed earlier in this chapter, we might conclude that same-sex role models are necessary. However, as gender-role theory has evolved, identification has progressively been de-emphasized as an important factor in sex typing, although imitation and observational learning have remained (Huston, 1983). Moreover, Gerald Jones (1990) has suggested that, "despite wide-spread popular beliefs, there is little research to verify the notion that girls and boys need same-sex role models for optimum development" (p. 9). The empirical evidence reviewed here supports his conclusion by showing that the differences between children in single-mother and two-parent children are small and probably of little practical importance.

Jones (1990) also suggested that in western culture, boys tend to model their behavior on abstract, media-propagated male images, whereas girls more often have contact with mothers and other real people as mentors and role models. We believe that children benefit from predictable relationships with well-adjusted, caring adults, regardless of gender or kinship, and that such relationships should be fostered regardless of the child's family structure. We also suggest that the gender of the adult matters only insofar as he or she is an exemplar of the category *man* or *woman* and to some degree contributes to the development of gender schema. If children encounter men and women in a variety of roles, they will develop schema that allow them to fulfill their own potentials rather than to be bound by rigid roles.

Overview

Differences in sex-typed behavior between offspring of single- and two-parent families are small or nonexistent.

Little research is currently being done in this area. Although decreased research interest in these effects may be the result of the minimal magnitude of the findings, it is more likely the result of changes in the value of sex-typed behavior in our culture. Over the last two decades, the rigidity of gender schema has lessened. Women are now better represented in the work force, and men are expected to be more involved in the family. Although researchers have become less enamored with the construct (Stevenson, 1991; Taylor & Hall, 1982), psychological androgyny, that is, possession of both masculine and feminine attributes, is still a valued ideal. Research has demonstrated that neither sex-typed behavior nor androgyny consistently predicts differences in mental health. Generally, masculinity scales, which typically measure instrumental personality characteristics, are better predictors of adjustment than femininity scales or a combination of masculinity and femininity (Dusek, 1987; Whitley, 1983, 1985).

Some have suggested (e.g., Parke, 1981) that sons of single mothers are better off than sons in two-parent families because they are less sex-stereotypical. However, this overgeneralization must be avoided. It is more appropriate to conclude that the effects of single mothering are limited and of little consequence in offsprings' lives.

Summary

- Most theories predict that a resident father is necessary for appropriate gender-role development, and that this is particularly true for boys.
- A meta-analysis of the literature concerning sex typing of offspring and family structure showed that the differences between offspring in one- and two-parent families are small for boys and practically nonexistent for girls.

- Although the effects do appear to be influenced by age and race, the quality of the data prohibits more specific conclusions.
- Children will benefit from good relationships with mentally healthy adults, regardless of the gender of the adult or the child and regardless of family structure.

7

Romantic Relationships

CHAPTER OUTLINE

Preview

Current literature provides evidence relevant to numerous interrelated questions concerning the relation between disruption of familial relationships due to divorce and offsprings' beliefs about and behaviors in romantic relationships. Unlike the other topics discussed, the overwhelming majority of studies has focused on females. Most often, the disruption of the father-child relationship is inferred from the divorce and from the father's absence from the home. However, recent studies have attempted to assess offsprings' perceptions regarding the quality of their father-child relationship.

Theoretical Predictions and Methodological Limitations

Various theoretical positions argue that parental divorce will affect the development of romantic and sexual relationships among offspring. Theoreticians have speculated that divorce and subsequent father absence may lead to difficulty in forming heterosexual relationships (Biller, 1974; Hetherington & Deur, 1971), to a lack of trust in the stability of marital relationships, to profound fears of marital failure (Sorosky, 1977), and to considerable conflict in developing sexual relationships (Sorosky, 1977; Westman, 1972). Wallerstein (1991) suggests that, "The developmental task of establishing intimacy and relationship with the opposite [sic] sex is . . . persistently burdened to a greater or lesser degree by the template of the failed-man-woman relationship that these youngsters carry within them" (p. 358).

Girls are regarded as particularly vulnerable because interacting with a warm but masculine father is presumed to contribute to the daughter's ability to interact appropriately with male peers. Daughters without fathers (as is assumed with divorce) would have difficulty learning how to interact with men. In addition, the spousal relationship may teach the child about the nature of intimate relationships or provide a model of an adult male-female relationship, both of which are likely to affect the child's relationships later in life (Goldenberg & Goldenberg, 1985). Kalter (1987) has suggested that girls identify with their mothers and that following divorce, "identifications with mother carry with them a pervasive and painful sense of having been inadequate and unloved in a centrally important heterosexual relationship" (p. 597).

The most recent theoretical development in this area provides an evolutionary perspective on these relations (Belsky, Steinberg, & Draper, 1991). This model suggests that the parental discord, stress, and inadequate financial resources that can accompany divorce may lead to harsh, rejecting, and inconsistent parenting. Ineffective child-rearing practices are expected to result in insecure attachments, a sense of mistrust in the environment, and an opportunistic interpersonal orientation. Taken together, these processes lead to early pubertal development. Early maturation is expected to lead to earlier sexual activity, short-term, unstable heterosexual relationships, and limited investment in parenting.

In contrast to other areas of research on single mothering, and consistent with theoretical expectations, relevant case studies are more likely to focus on daughters than on sons. Some case studies demonstrate a relation between paternal absence and difficulties in heterosexual adjustment for daughters (Eisendorfer, 1943; Gay & Tonge, 1967; Heckel, 1963; Keiser, 1953; Leonard, 1966). However, at least one attempt to support the hypothesis failed (Trunnell, 1968). Case reports on male offspring are more likely to focus on other aspects of gender-role development (Gay & Tonge, 1967; Meiss, 1952; Zients, 1986).

This wealth of clinical material also shows that paternal absence is often associated with other potentially hazardous experiences, many of which were related to the quality of the parent-child relationships. Mothers were described as openly seductive (Keiser, 1953) and as immature, dependent, and insecure (Heckel, 1963). Keiser (1953) suggested that an unreliable father, who continuously promised to return but never did, contributed to his daughter's maladjustment. Eisendorfer (1943) suggested that a child's emotional bond with the remaining parent might become too intense. Kestenbaum and Stone (1976) observed that among their cases, the healthiest daughters had better mothers.

In their study interviewing children of divorce, Wallerstein and Kelly (1974) reported that their original sample of offspring whose parents had recently divorced included adolescents who expressed concern about the success of their future marriages. Some said that they would never marry; others said that they were determined to make better choices of marital partners, and would marry later. At the 10-year follow up (Wallerstein, 1985a,b), many were still concerned about choosing their marital partners carefully, were eager for lasting marriages, but indicated that they were not going to be impulsive and might live with the person first, and that they would delay having children until certain that the relationship would last. However, a significant minority of females was wary of commitment, fearful of betrayal, and had experienced a series of short-lived sexual relationships.

Again, case studies and intensive interviews provide useful qualitative data, but are inappropriate as a basis for generalizations about the influence of single parenting. Unfortunately, much of the extant literature addressing the relation between single mothering and the offspring's subsequent romantic relationships consists of theoretical and speculative discussions supported by case histories and a few, often-cited studies. The studies are often characterized by problems seen before in research on the consequences of parental divorce on offspring: Father absence has a variety of meanings, and participants whose fathers are absent for different reasons are often lumped together. This can be significant; in some theoretical approaches there should be a difference between those who have never known their father and those whose relationship with their father was disrupted (Kestenbaum & Stone, 1976). Sometimes the research reports do not indicate which parent was absent (Gay & Tonge, 1967). In addition, the length of the absence can vary from a few months to many years and is often unspecified.

In spite of the limitations related to research design, we will report on the available literature that has attempted to answer the major questions in this area.

Interactions with Members of the Other Gender

The study that has received the most attention and been heralded as a model of good methodology (Santrock & Madison, 1985) was published in 1972 by E. Mavis Hetherington. Hetherington presented evidence, gathered from interviews with adolescent girls, that both daughters of divorcees and daughters of widows felt insecure around male peers and adults. However, this insecurity was displayed behaviorally in very different ways. Daughters of divorcees displayed more attention-seeking from males, whereas daughters of widows appeared to avoid interaction with males. From ratings of nonverbal behaviors, Hetherington concluded that daughters of single mothers differed in their manner of interaction with male interviewers.

> Daughters of widows demonstrated relatively infrequent speech and eye contact, avoidance of proximity with the interviewer in seat selection and body orientation and rigid postural characteristics. In contrast, daughters of divorcees again showed proximity seeking and a smiling, open, receptive manner with the male interviewer. (p. 323–324)

To have a homogeneous sample and control for extraneous variables, only girls whose fathers had left (by death or divorce) early in the daughter's lives, whose mothers were not dating, and who had no adult males living in the home were included. This is obviously an unusual sample.

This study is often cited in general summaries and in child development and introductory psychology textbooks. Unfortunately, other studies that provide evidence bearing on this issue contradict Hetherington's findings and rarely appear in the general sources. Hainline and Feig (1978) attempted to replicate Hetherington's (1972) observations in a sample of college women but found no differences in the behavior of women in the two groups. Furthermore, Young and Parish (1977) studied college women who had experienced either parental divorce or death, comparing willingness to associate with the other gender, and found no differences. Bannon and Southern (1980) compared college women from one- and two-parent families on sociability, aggressiveness, and nurturance toward peer-age men. The only significant difference showed that females from single-parent families were less nurturant toward male peers. Finally, parental divorce does not appear to be related to intimacy with partners for college women (Burstein, 1983) or for young adult men (Guttman, 1989).

These contradictions may be explained in a number of ways. Hetherington's findings may only apply to a specific group of adolescent females who have little experience with boys or men. By the time these adolescents reach college age, they may have learned to interact with males in more conventional ways. Alternatively, as discussed in chapter 5, perhaps college women who have experienced parental divorce are unrepresentative of the general population of daughters of divorce. Finally, perhaps social forces have changed so much in the last 20 years that these findings no longer apply to single-parent offspring.

Dating

Several studies have considered whether offspring of single parents differ from those of two-parent families in their dating or courtship behaviors. Studies of adolescents (Griggs, 1968; Nelson & Vangen, 1971; Hetherington, 1972) and of college students (Andrews & Christensen, 1951; Greenberg & Nay, 1982; Hepworth, Ryder, & Dreyer, 1984; Kalter, Riemer, Brickman, & Chen, 1985; Robson, 1983; Stevenson, 1991; Winch, 1949) provide little evidence that offspring of single parents differ dramatically from those of two parents in their dating activities. However, some of these studies combined offspring of parental divorce with those of parental death. There is some evidence suggesting that offspring of divorced couples differ from others, especially from those who have experienced parental death (Black & Sprenkle, 1991; Hetherington, 1972; Hepworth, Ryder, & Dreyer, 1984). These studies conclude that offspring of divorced parents may have a greater number of partners and become involved at slightly younger ages, whereas offspring of parental death are more likely to become involved in fewer relationships of longer duration and a more serious nature. In contrast, Greenberg and Nay (1982) showed that those whose parent had died were less involved in heterosexual relationships than were those from two-parent, never-divorced families.

■_____

Life Story

Gus

Gus was the third of three children of Peter and Diane. His brother is two years older, and his sister is five years older. Peter was a successful businessman in Washington state, and Diane was a housewife during their marriage. Although the children do not remember much conflict prior to the separation, they do recall that Peter was an unusually strict disciplinarian who often yelled and sometimes "belted" them. However, war broke out when Gus was 4, and Diane decided to separate. Each parent accused the other of infidelity, Gus believes, accurately. There were personal and legal arguments over division of property; Peter went to court asking for custody of the children. Although Gus was aware of what was occurring, he tended to isolate himself psychologically from the slamming doors and just went on playing. The children, who wanted to stay with their mother, were outside the courtroom when it was decided that Diane would have custody and that Peter would have visitation on alternate weekends and for six weeks in the summer. Although Diane and Peter have not talked to one another since this time, they have not tried to involve the children in any further disputes. Peter did pay support, and visitation occurred. Peter married the woman with whom he had been involved, and this marriage lasted three years.

Diane went back for trade school training in order to be employable. They moved to another house. For the first time, the children had chores; each did whatever was needed, and either a boy or girl might do cooking or yard work. Their mother took time to explain why things were different and why they saw so much less of her. Gus remembers that his brother was more resistant than the other two and that he also had some problems in school. Gus did well in school and believes that academics were a way for him to escape from thinking about any problems at home. He also became very involved in sports and thinks that being physical is a good way for him to vent his frustrations.

When Gus was in high school, Diane married Wayne, who had four children from a previous marriage. These children, all older than Gus, sometimes visited on weekends and in the summers. Gus is glad that his mother has finally found happiness.

Gus sees himself, and his friends agree, as an easygoing guy who adjusts to situations well. He does not remember crying at any time about the divorce and thinks that being together with his older siblings helped him adjust to missing his father. He presently seems to have congenial but not especially intimate relationships with his siblings. Congenial would also describe the way he gets along with his present stepparents. Gus has four stepsiblings from his mother's remarriage; he wishes that they could have become more of an integrated family. He would like to get to know his second stepmother, who is of another race, and thinks that he'd also like to meet her children from a prior marriage, who are adults with children of their own.

In a college fraternity now, Gus's goal is to have a good time, earn a degree, and become an engineer. Although Gus dates frequently, he has never had a serious relationship. He is apprehensive of commitment, but is not sure that this stems from the divorce. Gus believes that his parents' divorce was for the best, and that everyone has adjusted and is happier. Nonetheless, when he eventually marries, Gus wants it to be for life, so that the three children that he plans will experience the happiest childhood possible.

Attitudes about Sex and Sexual Activity

Studies focusing on the attitudes of offspring of divorce toward sex have produced inconsistent results. Among lower-class female teens (Eberhardt & Schill, 1984) or among Caucasian college women (Burstein, 1983; Hainline & Feig, 1978) some show few group differences that could be related to parental divorce. However, one large-scale study of Caucasian 18-year-olds indicated that offspring whose mothers were remarried were more accepting of premarital sex than were children of divorced mothers or never-married mothers (Thornton & Camburn, 1987). A study of adult women who responded to a newspaper ad showed that daughters of divorce were more open and comfortable about sex, or were more likely to have an experimental attitude toward sexual matters, than were women from two-parent families (Van Bergen, 1979). A study of college students showed that men whose parents divorced were the most permissive in their attitudes toward sexual behavior, women whose parents divorced were the most conservative, and those from non-divorced families fell in between. These findings must be considered with caution, however, because the return rate for questionnaires from the men was low, which may have skewed the findings (Billingsham, Pillion, & Sauer, 1991).

With a few exceptions (Eberhardt & Schill, 1984; Michael & Tuma, 1985), studies of both African-American and Caucasian noncollege samples show that offspring of divorce are more likely than offspring of two parents to experience greater sexual intimacy, to have had a number of different sexual partners, to have premarital births, to have multiple adolescent pregnancies, and to have their first child earlier (Gispert, Brinich, Wheeler, & Krieger, 1984; Haurin, 1992; Hetherington & Parke, 1979; Hogan & Kitagawa, 1985; Illsley & Thompson, 1961; McLanahan & Bumpass, 1988; Mueller & Cooper, 1986; Stern, Northman, & Van Slyck, 1984; Thornton & Camburn, 1987). Surbey (1990) provided a biosocial explanation for these findings, arguing that early absence of the father and the stress related to parental divorce leads girls to reach sexual maturity (menarche) earlier than girls in non-divorced families.

Although daughters of divorce who attend college may become sexually active at an earlier age than women from two-parent families (Kinnard & Gerrard, 1986; Musser, 1982), with few exceptions (e.g., Billingsham, Pillion, & Sauer, 1991), there are essentially no group differences in the present sexual activity of female or male college students that could be attributed to parental divorce (Belcastro & Nicholson, 1989; Hainline & Feig, 1978; Hepworth, Ryder, & Dreyer, 1984; Musser, 1982; Robson, 1983; Stevenson, 1991). Maybe, due to economic and educational difficulties, many children of divorce, particularly those who marry or give birth early, never attend college; therefore, differences that are apparent among adolescents or noncollege youth may not appear in studies of college students.

Sexual Orientation

Both psychoanalytic and social learning theories predict that homosexuality should be more common among children reared in fatherless families (Golombok, Spencer, & Rutter, 1983). These theories have led to the conclusion that the "fatherlessness" which can result from divorce may lead to homosexuality in both sons and daughters (Adams, Milner, & Schrepf, 1984; Biller, 1974, 1993; Biller & Solomon, 1986). These conclusions were based on theoretical speculation or were generalizations based on retrospective data gathered from gay men and lesbians, many of whom were in therapy or analysis. Based on the debatable theoretical assumption that homosexual orientation is evidence of failure to achieve a masculine identity, Biller (1993; Biller & Solomon, 1986) essentially blames inadequate fathering for homosexual orientation in both sons and daughters. We could not find a single study that directly assessed the relation between parental divorce and an offspring's sexual orientation. Given the lack of evidence, and the fact that more recent theories concerning homosexuality do not rely on the assumption of failed masculine identity, there is no reason to believe that parental divorce increases the rate of homosexuality or heterosexuality.

Attitudes, Plans, and Predictions about Marriage

Most studies of attitudes toward marriage find few differences between offspring of different family forms among late adolescents (Ganong, Coleman, & Brown, 1981) or college students (Greenburg & Nay, 1982; Hainline & Feig, 1978; Long, 1983; Robson, 1983). However, one study of 13- and 14-year-olds (Paddock-Ellard & Thomas, 1981) and one of college women (Kinnard & Gerrard, 1986) found that offspring from non-divorced families held a more positive attitude toward marriage than did those from divorced families. In contrast, Livingston and Kordinak (1990) showed that males from divorced families held more egalitarian marital role expectations than did males from non-divorced families. There were no differences for females.

Recent studies have considered a college student's sense of trust in heterosexual relationships. Although most studies show that parental divorce was unrelated to a general sense of trust in relationships, in a current romantic partner, or in a hypothesized future spouse (Kirkpatrick, 1992; Franklin, Janoff-Bulman, & Roberts, 1990; Southworth & Schwarz, 1987), other studies describe offspring of divorce as less trustful of future spouses and less optimistic about the success of their own future marriages than offspring of never-divorced parents (Franklin, Janoff-Bulman, & Roberts, 1990; Kalter et al., 1985). Kirkpatrick (1992) suggests that these findings are more likely to be the result of parental infidelity and conflict rather than of divorce per se.

■ _____

Life Story

Shelly

Shelly is the only child of Bob and Pam. The family lives in Indiana in a largely rural area. Bob is a high school dropout who obtained a GED and who has for several decades been employed at the same factory as a machine operator. Pam, a high school graduate, has worked at various clerical positions, none for long periods of time. Shelly remembers going to her bedroom and shutting the door to escape the drinking and frequent verbal arguments over the years that preceded the separation when she was 8. The first time Shelly ever saw her father cry was when Bob and Pam were sitting on the living room couch, telling her of their plans to divorce. Shelly herself did a lot of crying after this and often asked her parents if they were going to get back together. She remembers with gratitude their openness in talking with her about what was going on. Following the separation, both parents drank more, and each was arrested once for drinking and driving. Neither parent has gone to counseling, although Shelly is conscious that her father asked her mother to go to marriage counseling, but Pam refused. The adults decided, without discussion with Shelly, that she would primarily stay with her mother, although there would be joint custody. Pam moved to a new house and Shelly switched schools. She remembers that weekend visitations with her father in the former family home were "ordinary, except that we talked a lot because there was just the two of us." Shelly had a hard time making friends at the new school and maintained her old friendships while visiting her father on weekends. By parental agreement, after one year Shelly returned to live with her father during the school year and with her mother during the summer. Suddenly, she became responsible for doing the dishes and helping out with household chores in general. Her father, who was recently forced to learn traditional women's tasks, "was always there, but he wanted me to learn to do things on my own." Shelly's major difficulty in living with her father had to do with his dating. She was jealous of any children that the women had and wanted verbal reassurance that no one could ever be as important to him as she was. Shelly still considered the bedroom to be "Mom and Dad's," and did not like it when Bob had someone spend the night. Her mother's dating was even more disturbing, as Pam would often leave Shelly with her grandparents, go to a bar, and then stay out all night. When Shelly was 14 years old, her mother remarried. Shelly's stepfather, Rick, and her mother fought frequently, both before and after the wedding. "I didn't like him before they got married, I didn't like him on the day of the wedding, I still don't like him. He's self-centered, doesn't treat my mom the way she deserves, and he's tried to take the place of my dad." Rick was previously married, and his three children from that marriage generally refuse to interact with him. Shelly does not really know them.

Concerns about her parents and their romantic interactions did not interfere with Shelly's functioning. She has followed rules at home and school (sometimes, she thinks, to her detriment). As a student she earned perfect attendance awards and was on the honor roll. Shelly generally avoids thinking about bad things in life, but has thought about her family situation over many years, finally reaching the conclusion that although she doesn't live with both of her parents, she still has a family and a mom and dad who love her as much as she loves them.

Presently 20 years old, Shelly is now a college undergraduate who wants to become a marriage and family therapist. When she returns to her hometown, she stays with her father and visits her mother and stepfather for several hours because she feels that she owes it to her mother. Shelly sometimes feels resentment toward her parents for not trying hard enough to make their marriage survive. She fears becoming involved in a relationship that will turn out like that of her parents and becomes tense whenever she anticipates an argument with anyone. Nonetheless, overall Shelly believes that her parents' divorce was for the best, and that the conflict would have continued, making everyone miserable. On the positive side, she believes that her father would not have become her best friend without the divorce.

Shelly has been dating the same hometown boy for two years and thinks that it might become serious. Before she marries, Shelly intends to cohabit and to have a prenuptial agreement requiring marriage counseling before separation is considered. She intends to wait several years after marriage before having a child.

Findings from studies that consider plans for marriage by offspring of divorce are not consistent. Some evidence suggests that fewer offspring of divorced parents plan to marry (Robson, 1983) and more plan to cohabitate (Southworth & Schwarz, 1987). Evidence also suggests that teenage marriages are more likely if parents divorced (McLanahan & Bumpass, 1988), and that single-parent girls marry earlier (Carlson, 1979). However, two studies showed no differences between offspring of divorce and those with parents who have not divorced in plans for marriage (Griggs, 1968; Guttman, 1989).

These contradictions may be the result of other variables influencing marriage beliefs and behaviors. For example, both Long (1983) and Landis (1962) showed that, in explaining offsprings' current beliefs, the happiness of the parents' marriage was more important than their divorce. In addition, lower educational attainment accounts to some degree for early marriages among offspring of divorce (Carlson, 1979; McLanahan & Bumpass, 1988).

Once married, there are only slight group differences in marital quality. Amato and Keith (1991b) reviewed 16 studies comparing adult offspring whose parents had divorced with offspring of never-divorced parents on measures of marital satisfaction, marital disagreements, and marital instability, and found a small but stable difference between the groups ($d = -.13$). Although those whose parents divorced are more likely to report having experienced marital problems, men from divorced backgrounds are also more likely to report high levels of harmony in their marriages. Perhaps offspring of divorce are more realistic in their assessments of marriage, because they report normative levels of happiness and more problems. Maybe they have a more sophisticated concept of marriage (Franklin, Janoff-Bulman, & Roberts, 1990) that allows them to report problems without feeling dissatisfied with the marriage (Kulka & Weingarten, 1979).

Attitudes toward and Likelihood of Divorce

The reason for differences in attitudes toward divorce has no clear answer. When comparing offspring from either married, divorced, or remarried families, sometimes no differences are reported (Black &

Sprenkle, 1991), sometimes offspring of divorce hold more favorable attitudes (Greenburg & Nay, 1982; Rozendal, 1983), sometimes offspring in non-divorced families hold more favorable attitudes (Paddock-Ellard & Thomas, 1981), and sometimes those in stepfamilies look more favorably toward divorce (Ganong, Coleman, & Brown, 1981; Kinnard & Gerrard, 1986).

In contrast, few question the finding that offspring of parents who divorced are more likely themselves to divorce (Black & Sprenkle, 1991; McLanahan & Bumpass, 1988; Mueller & Pope, 1977; Pope & Mueller, 1976). This process is sometimes referred to as intergenerational transmission. A meta-analysis (Amato & Keith, 1991b) of 24 studies showed that adults who experienced parental divorce as children were more likely to divorce ($d = -.22$) than were offspring of never-divorced parents. The relation between parent and offspring divorce is stronger for females than for males (Amato & Keith, 1991b; Bumpass & Sweet, 1972; Glenn & Shelton, 1983; Keith & Finlay, 1988; McLanahan & Bumpass, 1988), stronger among Caucasians than African Americans (Amato & Keith, 1991b; Glenn & Kramer, 1987), and stronger in the African-American middle class than in the lower class (Heiss, 1972).

Data from five major surveys (Pope & Mueller, 1976) showed that divorce rates among those whose parents had divorced were only modestly higher (5% to 12%) than among those from never-divorced families. The pattern of results varies somewhat depending on whom the child lived with after the divorce and whether remarriage occurred. For Caucasian females with siblings, those who lived with a single parent were less likely to have their first marriages end in divorce than were those whose mothers or fathers remarried. For Caucasian boys who lived with their mothers, remarriage was related to a decrease in the likelihood of subsequent divorce. Divorce rates for boys who had lived with their fathers were approximately the same, regardless of whether or not the father remarried. For Caucasians there was more transmission of marital instability for children who lived with their mothers rather than with their fathers, regardless of the sex of the offspring. Similar comparisons for African Americans yielded inconsistent findings. Furthermore, Heiss (1972) reported that the post-divorce living arrangement was not significantly related to later marital instability among African Americans.

Although there is support for the so-called "transmission hypothesis," there is also considerable debate about why offspring whose parents divorce are more likely to divorce. It has long been argued that this phenomenon could easily be explained through role modeling. However, evidence for this explanation is inconsistent. Furthermore, Catton (1988), argued that, based purely on whether parents are divorced or married, the proportion of offspring who divorce in subsequent generations should decrease. In other words, parental divorce alone cannot explain divorce among offspring.

Most likely, the relation between parental divorce and divorce among offspring is mediated by a variety of environmental factors (Pope & Mueller, 1976). Among Caucasians, much of the increase in likelihood of divorce may be explained by early marriages following parental divorce (Glenn & Kramer, 1987; Mueller & Pope, 1977). However, Michael and Tuma (1985) found early marriage to be related to living with a stepparent rather than with a single parent. It is unclear why some offspring of divorce marry early even though many say they intend to wait until they are older or intend to forego marriage (Wallerstein & Kelly, 1974). Economic factors may be more important than parental marital status for some. However, the evidence is inconsistent (Glenn & Kramer, 1987).

In contrast, McGue and Lykken (1992) argued that this increased risk of divorce is unlikely to be the result of environmental factors alone. Their data show that concordance for divorce was significantly higher in monozygotic than in dizygotic twins, demonstrating that genetic factors may play a role.

Overview

Strong conclusions concerning many of these issues are difficult to support. Obviously, however, the differences between offspring of divorce and offspring with married parents are not nearly as clear-cut or as consistent as we would expect from theory.

In spite of evidence demonstrating some small differences between offspring of divorced and non-divorced parents, these differences do not necessarily indicate maladjustment and could in some ways be viewed as more complex, more realistic, or more adaptive. Furthermore, the extent to which these differences should be attributed to parental divorce is unclear. This relation may be mediated by a variety of variables, both environmental and genetic.

Differences in the attitudes and behaviors of adolescents from divorced and non-divorced families are sometimes replicated with non-college samples of young adults. However, they are rarely replicated in college samples. Offspring whose parents divorced and who attend college probably differ systematically from those who do not. For example, in the past, the lower social classes—the poor and less educated—were more likely to have premarital sex and early intercourse. The difference between the classes is decreasing, but still exists. Logically, when groups of those from divorced or non-divorced families are compared, there will be differences in social class background; therefore, the overall finding of more early sexual behavior among the children of divorce may reflect the fact that there are more of them from the lower socioeconomic class and because lower-class youth are less likely to attend college. Therefore, it is not surprising to find few differences in college samples.

It is likely that a subset of those who experience parental divorce behave differently in their subsequent relationships when compared to offspring of never-divorced parents. In some instances, offspring may model the behavior or attitudes of their parents. For example, early sexual experiences of offspring of divorce may be the result of knowing that their parents are single, dating, and sexually active (Thornton & Camburn, 1987). Children in traditional two-parent homes rarely become aware that their parents are sexually active. Alternatively, parents who divorce may not be able to supervise their children because they are at work and cannot afford supervision. It is reasonable to assume that adolescents are more likely to become sexually active when they can find the time and a place to do so with no one telling them that they cannot.

The variables of parental conflict and the quality of the father-child relationship may be important mediators in findings in this area as well. Children from never-divorced, happy homes threaten to break up relationships less often than children of either divorced or non-divorced, unhappy homes (Booth, Brinkerhoff, & White, 1984). Furthermore, in a study of pregnant daughters in never-divorced families, parental discord led to the deterioration of the father-daughter relationship. Such marriages produced daughters who had greater numbers of partners, who were more likely to be unmarried and without plans for marriage, who more often did not live with the father of the child, and who expressed greater dissatisfaction with their current partner (Uddenberg, 1976). These data suggest that it may not be parental divorce that is problematic, but the combination of parental discord and a poor relationship with the father.

A recent study of college students (Stevenson, 1991) focused on the effects of parental conflict, closeness in the father-offspring relationship, and parental divorce upon offsprings' subsequent development of heterosexual relationships. The major finding was that when parental conflict and closeness of the father-child relationship were taken into account, parental marital status was not associated with the quality of the offspring's heterosexual relationships. The emotional tenor of offspring's romantic relationships had more to do with the amount of conflict in relationships between the parents than whether a divorce had occurred. This suggests that studies simply comparing single-mother offspring with offspring in never-divorced, two-parent homes, without considering other mediating variables, may overestimate the extent to which these outcomes should be attributed to divorce per se, or to living with the mother.

These data and others in the empirical literature concerning romantic relationships again remind us that we must focus on dynamic processes and not structure.

Summary

- Theoretically, offspring of divorce, particularly daughters, should have more difficulties in their romantic relationships than offspring of two parents.
- Much of the research concerning the relation between parental divorce and offsprings' romantic relationships is inconsistent.
- Offspring of divorce do become involved in sexual relationships earlier than offspring in non-divorced families.
- Contrary to theoretical predictions, there is no apparent relation between sexual orientation and parental divorce.
- Generally, there are few differences in attitudes about marriage between offspring of divorced and those of non-divorced parents. However, parental divorce may be related to an offspring's sense of trust in future partners and general satisfaction with a marital relationship.
- Offspring of divorce are somewhat more likely than offspring of non-divorced parents to divorce themselves. This is probably due to earlier marriage and to economic factors rather than to role modeling.
- Differences between offspring of divorced and those of non-divorced parents may be attributed to parental discord and poor relationships with parents rather than to divorce.

Antisocial Behavior

Preview

As noted earlier, some young children, especially boys, become aggressive, at least for a time, following parental separation (Stevenson & Black, 1988). Offspring of divorce are also over-represented in samples of children referred for counseling or therapy because of antisocial and aggressive behavior (Tuckman & Regan, 1966). This behavior often bothers parents and school personnel and can end up involving the legal system.

In this chapter, we consider the relation between parental divorce and "antisocial" behaviors, including conduct problems, drug use, running away, and shoplifting, among others. Many of these behaviors are conventionally classified as "juvenile delinquency." Because some of these misbehaviors can be interpreted as indicators of lower levels of moral development, we will briefly consider the meager literature on the relation between family structure and moral development.

Conduct and Behavior Disorders

A meta-analysis found that the difference between offspring of divorce and those in non-divorced families was larger for conduct problems (including aggression, delinquency, and other misbehavior) than for any other area except that of relations between fathers and children (Amato & Keith, 1991a). The extent of conduct problems was greater in data collected prior to 1970. Significant differences were found for both males and females and at all ages up to college. A second meta-analysis of research on adults whose parents had divorced years earlier (Amato & Keith, 1991b) included behavior and conduct problems as one category. There were significant differences between these grown offspring and those from families who had remained married. However, the majority of the studies had used samples obtained in clinical settings; further, such studies yielded larger negative effects than did studies with nonclinical populations.

Using a nationwide sample of children between 4 and 16 years of age, a recent study (Achenbach, McConaughy, & Howell, 1987) assessed problems as reported by at least one parent. Children of never-married or separated/divorced parents had higher total problem scores than where parents were married to each other, or when a parent was widowed. Almost 30 percent of those whose parents were separated or divorced had problem scores above the eightieth percentile. When more related adults lived in the household, problem scores were reduced. This finding did not occur for unrelated adults. The authors suggested that the presence of related adults in the household may provide psychological support of some kind that could ameliorate potential problems.

Taken together, the evidence suggests that the majority of offspring of divorce will not show behavior problems; however, as compared to the general population, a greater proportion of both male and female offspring of divorce will have some overt inappropriate behaviors. More examination of other variables, possibly associated with variations in this proportion, is needed. For example, maybe behavior disorders, as many other outcomes, are mediated by parental conflict or by economic stress.

Use of Controlled Substances

Recent studies have demonstrated a relation between family structure and substance use among offspring (e.g., Haurin, 1992). A study of 7,426 middle and secondary school students showed that living in a nontraditional family was related in varying degrees to use of tobacco, alcohol, marijuana, cocaine, inhalants, narcotics, hallucinogens, and over-the-counter drugs (Nelson, Thompson, Rice, & Cooley, 1991). Using a stage model of drug use, Brook, Whiteman, and Gordon (1985) reported that in their sample of 15- and 16-year-old African-American and Caucasian males and females, offspring of divorce were likely to report higher stages of drug use. The model describes four stages: (1) no drug use; (2) use of licit drugs; (3) marijuana use; and (4) use of other illicit drugs. Two studies of substance abuse were carried out in Minnesota, with a sample consisting largely of Caucasian and well-educated families. Adolescent children reported on their usage of illicit substances such as alcohol, marijuana, or cocaine. A composite score of usage frequency during the last year was computed. Those adolescents whose parents had recently divorced were more likely to be substance users than those whose parents had divorced prior to adolescence or whose parents were still married (Needle, Su, & Doherty, 1990). Further analyses (Doherty & Needle, 1991) showed that the increase in substance use was greater for boys than for girls in the families disrupted by divorce. This may be a reflection of the greater likelihood of acting out behavior on the part of stressed males.

These studies show that some offspring of divorce were more likely to use drugs than were offspring from non-divorced families, but that the data do not reveal why the adolescents used drugs. Kalter (1984) has noted in a clinical report that alcohol involvement occurred with troubled adolescent daughters of divorce and suggested that the increase in drinking might be associated with excessive use of alcohol by parents. We might also speculate that stressed adolescents use drugs as an escape or as a coping strategy.

■_____

Life Story

Gladys

Gladys, now 38 years of age, experienced parental divorce when it was still relatively uncommon. Before Gladys was born, her mother, Peggy, had been twice married and divorced and had two children. She married Gladys' father, Charlie, when Gladys was a few weeks old. Three other children were born in the next four years. Gladys' earliest memories are of violent conflicts between her parents. Charlie was diagnosed as paranoid schizophrenic and was committed to a mental hospital for three years. Gladys' mother was on antidepressant medication for most of this time. At the age of 5, Gladys was changing diapers. When she entered school she was fixing breakfast for six children while her mother, who worked nights, was sleeping. When she was 9, she hauled laundry to the laundromat in a wagon; her mother paid her a penny a piece for doing the ironing. Peggy gave up for adoption the two older children, Gladys' older siblings, whom she had been mothering; then Peggy divorced Charlie and was awarded custody of their four children. However, unable to care for them herself, she left them with friends in another city for a year. They were then placed in a private Catholic "orphanage" for three years when Gladys was in elementary school. Peggy eventually married for the fourth time, reclaimed the children, and took them to Chicago. Gladys' stepfather, Herb, was an alcoholic who sometimes made sexual advances to her which she successfully repelled. Chicago winters were cold and windy. For boots, the children wore plastic sandwich wrap with rubber bands around the ankles. Gladys, the oldest remaining child, remembers helping her mother steal food and going to a nearby shrimp house to beg for leftovers at the end of the evening. Finally, Herb went into an alcohol-induced psychosis. Peggy separated from him. The children were sent to live with various grandparents, aunts, and uncles in the next years. Their father had been appearing inconsistently for unsupervised visits, which upset the children, as he spent the time telling them how awful their mother was; he appeared irrational and on the verge of breakdown. During this time, one of Gladys' sisters was killed in an accident. When Gladys was 16, her mother was paralyzed in a one-car, alcohol-related accident. Her father was neither willing nor able to provide a home. The three children became wards of the court. Before she reached the age of 18, Gladys had been in four different foster homes, separated from her sisters. Before graduating from high school, she had attended ten different schools. Gladys did not do well in school, perhaps because of the many moves. Other factors were that Gladys was dyslexic and often ill from severe allergies and asthmas.

One of Gladys' coping mechanisms was to take someone under her wing for protection. This included not only her siblings but also friends when she was in a place long enough to make a friend. Her closest friends when growing up were a girl with epilepsy and one who was grossly obese. She became close to her friends' parents and obtained sympathy and comfort from these adults. Gladys began romantic relationships with sexual activity while still in high school. She now believes that she was copying her mother's behaviors, as she became involved with males who were abusive both physically and psychologically. Gladys remained with men who slapped her or who were with her one week and another woman the next.

In her effort not to be a burden on anyone, Gladys avoided any problem behavior until after she was an adult; then, she was fired from several jobs, she experimented with drugs, and she was intermittently anorexic and ate little. Because of contraceptive failure, Gladys' sexual behavior resulted first in an abortion and then a child out of wedlock. Gladys married a man who kicked her in the stomach when she was five months pregnant. A subsequent difficult pregnancy and delivery resulted in a partial hysterectomy. When the marriage was coming to an end, Gladys began to drink. Unable to work and support the children, she gave them up for adoption at the encouragement of a welfare worker. Her life went out of control and she drifted, continuing to drink for about three years. Although the severe drinking ceased, Gladys continued in abusive relations and experienced frequent depressions for about ten years. After both of her parents died, Gladys' depression improved. Interestingly, for the last 5 years of her life, the mother-child relationship had reversed in that Peggy had called Gladys "mother." Gladys is able to articulate both her sympathy for her parents and her resentment of their behaviors. However, her major resentment is focused on the welfare and legal systems that she feels failed her, both when she was a child of divorce and when going through divorce herself.

At some point, Gladys made the deliberate decision that she did not want to look into a mirror and see someone who was like her mother; she stopped interacting with inappropriate males. She met Glenn and after living with him for three years and making sure that he was reliable and healthy, they married. She has now been happily married for seven years. One of her regrets is that they will never have children.

Gladys would like to have had models other than her parents and relatives; or that someone had sent her to counseling when she was growing up. She is determined never to be a victim again. Having decided that "the only way women can make themselves powerful is to get the best education they can get," Gladys has returned to college. Her goal is to earn a degree that will enable her to help disturbed or abused children.

One of the most dramatic changes in Gladys' life occurred recently when she was able to locate her oldest child, who is now 18. A meeting with her daughter, a freshman in college, was a happy one, and they will remain in contact.

Juvenile Delinquency

The best evidence concerning the relation between parental divorce and misconduct comes from two meta-analyses. One (Amato & Keith, 1991a) reviewed 56 studies of children and showed that offspring of divorce were more likely to misbehave or be delinquent than were offspring of never-divorced parents ($d = -.23$). The other (Amato & Keith, 1991b) reviewed nine studies of adults who had experienced parental divorce as children and found that offspring of divorce were more likely to engage in criminal behavior, drug use, alcoholism, suicide, and the like when compared to offspring of never-divorced parents ($d = -.28$).

The differences shown in the meta-analyses are rather small. Furthermore, understanding the relationship between parental divorce and delinquent behavior in offspring is difficult for a number of reasons. This literature usually focuses on "broken homes" that typically include any family structure that does not consist of a male and a female adult who are the biological parents of the offspring (what we refer to as the *traditional family*). Sometimes stepfamilies are considered "broken" and sometimes they are not. In some instances, homes that are broken for a variety of reasons are treated as though they were all the result of divorce (Wilkinson, 1980). Few attempts have been made to differentiate between the various alternative family forms. The few studies that have considered offspring of divorce specifically showed that higher rates of delinquency are more likely in this group than in families broken by parental death (Gibson, 1969; Gregory, 1965; Rutter & Madge, 1976). Given the derogatory connotations of the term "broken home," we will refer to them as "nontraditional" families.

A second problem concerns how "juvenile delinquency" is defined and how generalizations are made. What has been referred to as "juvenile delinquency" encompasses a variety of defining characteristics including truancy, running away, theft, engaging in premarital sexual behavior, arrests, residence in a home for delinquents, and so on. Sometimes studies use aggregate measures including a variety of behaviors; sometimes a single behavior is used. When offspring of nontraditional homes are found to be more likely than other offspring to engage in any of these behaviors, it is often assumed that they are also more likely to engage in other delinquent behaviors (Hennessy, Richards, & Berk, 1978). One might well question the accuracy of such an assumption. Rankin (1983) suggests that residing in nontraditional homes may be positively related to some acts of delinquency, unrelated to others, and negatively associated with still others. For example, running away, truancy, fighting, and auto theft have been shown to be related to residence in a nontraditional home (Browning, 1960; Rankin, 1983), although the incidence of some of these behaviors was even greater in stepfamilies. In contrast, family context has been shown to be unrelated to vandalism, theft, trespass, auto theft, entry, assault, or threat (Rankin, 1983; Dentler & Monroe, 1961).

Studies of nontraditional families and delinquency have most often used data gathered from police records or samples of those who have come into the court system, and have compared the family histories of these groups with others who are assumed to be nondelinquent youth (Andrews, 1976; Gibson, 1969; Offord, Abrams, Allen, & Poushinsky, 1979; Smith & Walters, 1978). Based on such data, many have long believed that the nontraditional home was an important antecedent to delinquent behavior (Hennessy, Richards, & Berk, 1978; Rosen, 1970; Rutter & Madge, 1976), even though many of these studies show only small differences (Adams, Milner, & Schrefp, 1984; Rosen & Neilson, 1982), and the vast majority of those from nontraditional homes were not delinquent. For example, in a British sample, 19 percent of "officially" delinquent boys were from families that experienced divorce or death, whereas 12 percent of nondelinquent boys were from such families (Power, Ash, Shoenberg, & Sirey, 1974).

Official statistics do suggest that delinquents are more likely to come from nontraditional homes. However, these data may reflect differential treatment by the authorities as much as they are indicators of the offender's behavior (Hennessy et al., 1978). Juvenile justice agencies routinely include the stability of the home as a criterion for legal intervention (Farnworth, 1984). Court records, then, are likely to contain biases due to both race and family background (Hampton, 1975; Thomas & Sieverdes, 1975), and are a better indicator of juvenile authorities' reactions to illegal behavior than they are of actual offense patterns (Rankin, 1983). For example, local authorities may be more likely to give the offspring of a traditional home the benefit of the doubt or to allow the parents (particularly the father) to provide disciplinary action; a single mother living in poverty would be assumed to need the help of the authorities in providing appropriate discipline for her children. As a result, more offspring of nontraditional homes would end up in the official statistics.

In addition to reports based on official statistics, data have been gathered using anonymous self-report questionnaires of representative samples. In a national probability sample of adolescents, Canter (1982) found that youths from nontraditional homes engaged in significantly more delinquent acts in a variety of forms than did youths from traditional homes. In contrast, three other studies have found that the relation between residence in nontraditional homes and specific delinquent behaviors is weak or nonexistent (Hennessy et al., 1978; Levin, 1989; Rosen, 1970). Furthermore, using self-report measures, a 13-year longitudinal study in New Zealand found strong support for the hypothesis that exposure to parental discord leads to increased risk of early offending, whereas exposure to changes in family structure in the absence of discord does not (Ferguson, Horwood, & Lynskey, 1992).

Sex Differences

Regardless of whether criminal statistics or self-report measures are used (Rutter & Madge, 1976), delinquent behavior is more common among boys than girls in all broad categories, even though the same variables are thought to explain the propensity toward delinquency for both sexes (Smith, 1979). However, some experts have suggested that familial relationships are more important to the development of girls than boys; therefore, they predict that delinquent behavior is more likely to result for girls from nontraditional homes than for boys. Interestingly, some studies of delinquents show that girls from nontraditional homes are more likely than boys to become delinquent (Andrews, 1976; Cockburn & Maclay, 1965; Monahan, 1957; Offord et al., 1979; Toby, 1957), whereas others do not (Berger & Simon, 1974; Canter, 1982; Chilton & Markle, 1972; Farnworth, 1984; Hennessy et al., 1978; Wilkinson, 1980).

Explanations for this inconsistency abound. The obtained sex difference could be an artifact related to the differences between official statistics and self-reports of delinquent behavior (Canter, 1982), or the difference may depend on the type of offense involved. Higher arrest rates for certain offenses may result from more stringent social sanctions for girls and may simply be a statistical artifact associated with the type of delinquency for which boys and girls are usually arrested or referred to court (Rankin, 1983). For example, whereas Rankin's (1983) survey data showed that running away was equally likely in boys and girls, Datesman and Scarpitti (1975) showed that for those legally apprehended for running away, a nontraditional home was more likely in the background of females than males.

We see no reason to conclude that females are more likely than males to become delinquent following divorce. Furthermore, any generalization about the effect of gender may depend upon race, but the available data that address both race and gender are contradictory. Using court records, African-American males from nontraditional homes were more likely to engage in some forms of delinquency than were females, whereas the opposite was true for Caucasians (Datesman & Scarpitti, 1975). In contrast, Austin (1978), using a stratified probability sample, found no relation between single mothering and differences in theft, vandalism, and assault for African-American compared to Caucasian males. The relation between single mothering and theft was insignificant both for Caucasian boys and for Caucasian girls, although auto trespass and vandalism showed a significant relationship to single mothering among Caucasian girls. Using a probability sample, Berger and Simon (1974) reported that African-American female adolescents from two-parent families were more likely than those from one-parent families to be seriously involved in theft or violence and that nontraditional homes produced increases in delinquency only for working-class Caucasian males.

Race Differences

Researchers considering race differences in the effect of the nontraditional home on offspring have most often compared African-American and Caucasian offspring. We located only one study that considered another racial group. Wilkinson (1980) compared Mexican Americans with Caucasians and reported strikingly similar findings for boys in the two racial groups. However, Mexican-American girls from nontraditional homes were more likely to be arrested for shoplifting, auto theft, truancy, and running away; for Caucasians, girls were more likely to show drug use.

It has long been suggested that the relation between nontraditional homes and delinquency is greater among African Americans than among Caucasians (e.g., Matsueda & Heimer, 1987; Monahan, 1957; Moynihan, 1965), although the literature is inconsistent, with some finding no differences and others finding Caucasians to be more affected (Austin, 1978; Berger & Simon, 1974; Chilton & Markle, 1972; Rosen & Neilson, 1982; Tennyson, 1967; Toby, 1957). Clearly, findings from one racial group should not automatically be applied to another group who differ not only in racial category, but also in economic status.

Racial segregation often limits African Americans to inner-city neighborhoods with low socioeconomic status and favorable attitudes toward street crimes. Matsueda and Heimer (1987) argue that although the total effect of nontraditional homes on delinquency is larger for African American than for others, the same process influences delinquency in both racial groups. The absence of a parent lessens parental supervision and increases delinquent companions, predelinquent attitudes, and delinquent behavior. Perhaps even more importantly, nontraditional homes directly foster an excess of favorable attitudes to delinquency, which then increases delinquent behavior. Their data show that this attitudinal effect is much larger among African Americans and accounts for the greater total effect of nontraditional homes on fights, theft, and vandalism among African Americans.

As was the case in our consideration of sex differences in the impact of nontraditional homes on delinquency, the data on race differences do not allow for broad generalizations. Furthermore, it seems likely that economic, attitudinal, and methodological variables provide a better explanation than does racial category for the apparent race differences that are found.

Economic Differences

A history of welfare is more likely in divorced or other nontraditional families than in never-divorced families (Offord, et al., 1979). In understanding delinquency, a family's economic situation may be more important than its composition (Chilton & Markle, 1972).

In one study of African-American low-income youth, the important family characteristic was parental employment rather than family structure. Boys in homes where both parents were employed were less likely to run away or to use drugs than boys in other family groups that varied in parental marital and employment status. There were no effects for girls (Farnworth, 1984). In another study, the father's unemployment increased the likelihood of fighting or assault in both African-American and Caucasian adolescent boys, whereas the father's place of residence was unrelated (Brownfield, 1987).

One might also ask whether there are social class differences in the effects of a nontraditional home upon delinquent behaviors. Using court records, Gibson (1969) reported that homes affected by parental desertion, rather than by death, were especially associated with delinquency in boys and that this association was stronger in the more economically advantaged portion of the sample. Gibson speculated that those in lower classes were already at risk because of a myriad of other variables; thus, family structure was likely to have a greater impact on the middle or higher classes.

Causes of Juvenile Delinquency

Currently, professionals disregard divorce as a major variable in explaining juvenile delinquency. Potential mediators of the apparent relationship have been suggested. Wilkinson (1980) proposed that having a tolerant attitude toward divorce was an important mediator of the effects of divorce upon delinquent behavior; he believes that those who live in divorce-tolerant milieux should be less affected. Family size and lack of supervision or discipline have been suggested by a number of people (e.g., Rutter & Madge, 1976) as important predictors of delinquency. In addition, adolescents in single-parent homes may be more susceptible than those in non-divorced families to pressure from peers to engage in deviant behavior (Steinberg, 1987). Some argue that the relation between nontraditional homes and juvenile delinquency is not due to the marital break or to the absence of the father per se, but to stress in the situation (Power et al., 1974), or to the absence of a stable home environment.

The presence of parental pathology and general family discord are also relevant here. The relation between parental divorce and conduct disorder in boys could be the result of parental psychopathology. Antisocial personality in one of the parents could lead both to the divorce and to the son's conduct disorder (Lahey, Hartdagen, Frick, McBurnett, Connor, & Hynd, 1988). Maternal mental illness and paternal criminal behavior are more frequent in nontraditional homes, and parental personality problems are particularly important in delinquency production when they result in marital discord (Offord et al., 1979).

One may wonder why the father-absence paradigm, or the use of the "broken home" concept, persisted for so long as the major indicator of family disorganization. As early as 1960, Browning reported that adjustment or happiness in the parental marriage is much more closely related to delinquent behavior among adolescents than whether the marriage is an original marriage, a remarriage, or one in which the child was living with one parent. A number of studies over decades have found that delinquency is just as common among children from unhappy and quarrelsome married families as it is among those whose parents have divorced or separated (McCord & McCord, 1959; Power et al., 1974; Rutter & Madge, 1976). In addition, a higher proportion of gang delinquents is found among boys whose parents continued to live together despite considerable overt conflict than for those whose parents either were in little conflict or whose fathers were not living with them (McCord, McCord, & Thurber, 1962). Parental conflict is also related to recidivism; i.e., returns to court. In one study the largest percentage of persistent offenders (two or more court appearances and cautions) were from non-divorced families with severe problems (Power et al., 1974).

Moral Development

As mentioned earlier, persistent misconduct can be interpreted as an indicator of lower levels of moral development. In addition, Freudian theory predicts that boys without male role models will exhibit lower levels of moral development. Because the crucial variable is the absence of a father in the home, early research typically used samples mixing those whose fathers were dead and those living with their mothers after divorce. In comparison with children in two-parent homes, some research has found children whose fathers were not living with them to express lower levels of conscience development (Hoffman, 1971), and lower levels of moral reasoning (Daum & Bieliauskas, 1983). Two studies of moral reasoning with college students (Parish, 1980; Parish & Copeland, 1981) reported that the longer students had lived in a single-parent family, the lower their scores were. This finding should be viewed cautiously not only because of the small sample sizes, but also because there were no significant differences between one- and two-parent groups. In contrast, other researchers have found no differences in resistance to temptation (Mumbauer & Gray, 1970) and moral judgments that were related to the father's residence (Fry, 1983).

The most comprehensive study assessed moral development with 8 different sets of measures for behavior, judgment, and effect (Santrock, 1975), but found differences only on teacher's ratings of boys' moral behavior. One possibility is that differences are slight and would only be evidenced with sampling over a wide variety of instances, thus being reflected in teacher ratings but not from assessment in the laboratory. Alternatively, given that teachers are not unaware of their students' family backgrounds, these ratings could reflect teachers' negative expectations as much as they indicate differences in children's behavior.

Viewed overall, the literature on the relation between single mothering and measures specifically designed to assess moral development is inconclusive; if there are effects, they are probably not dramatic and may better be interpreted as misconduct or acting out rather than moral development. Interestingly, this area has not seen new research for some time, perhaps because the Freudian perspective on morality development is now less influential.

Overview

Following divorce, there is a greater likelihood that offspring will exhibit some acting out behaviors that will be disturbing to those around them and in some instances potentially harmful to the child. This includes an increase in physical aggression toward others, running away from home, and substance use. However, the available evidence does not allow us to conclude that divorce itself causes any of the possible differences in illegal or immoral behaviors between children who have and who have not experienced parental divorce. Rather, these differences may have preceded divorce, or some other factor other than divorce may be responsible.

Although one major goal of this chapter was to consider the impact of parental divorce on the development of delinquent behavior in offspring, much of the available data allow for discussion only of "broken" or nontraditional homes. The concept of the broken home carries many implications and assumptions that are no longer appropriate. Consideration of the literature reveals that experts often make broad generalizations about juvenile delinquency based on small differences in a specific behavior from a nonrepresentative sample of incarcerated youth or from "official statistics."

Because of the difficulty in separating the impact of correlated events and the inconsistency in research findings, it seems likely that parental divorce has little direct impact on delinquent behavior of offspring. Family discord and parental psychopathology appear to play a role in exacerbating delinquent behavior among offspring. Probably, however, much of the cause of delinquency comes from outside of the family (Power et al., 1974). Economic and attitudinal factors are important, also.

Unfortunately, although the current view among professionals is that the so-called broken home is only of secondary importance in illegal behaviors, the public may still regard divorce as a cause for delinquency (Rosen & Neilson, 1982). More accurate generalizations about specific matters in this field may be beneficial both in clarifying this belief and in informing public policy.

Summary

- The majority of offspring of divorce will not experience behavior problems.
- Offspring of divorce do appear more likely than offspring of non-divorced families to use controlled substances, but the data do not allow us to suggest why.
- Offspring in one-parent families are more likely to misbehave or be delinquent than offspring in two-parent families. However, the difference is small and is not likely to be the result of parental divorce per se.
- The available data do not consistently support generalizations concerning sex or race differences in the likelihood of delinquent behaviors as a result of parental divorce.
- Delinquent behavior is more likely the result of economic hardship, parental pathology, or conflict than of parental divorce.
- Research on the relation between moral development and parental divorce is inconclusive, although if there are effects, they are probably small.

9

Mental Health and Intervention

Preview

Although some researchers distinguish between short-term and long-term adjustment, there is no clear time period determining when long-term adjustment or effects begin. Researchers and clinicians in this field agree that almost all children will have some immediate negative reactions to the events surrounding separation and divorce and that these will last for a time ranging from months to a year or two. Interestingly, Heady and Wearing (1989) found that, for adults, some life events had an impact on subjective well-being for up to two years.

Research on mental health following divorce has recently emphasized a wide range of behaviors and attributes. Although some researchers use general measures of adjustment, others more specifically assess more limited constructs such as self-concept, locus of control, or depression. In this chapter we discuss numerous specific aspects of mental health, paying particular attention to the extent to which these effects are short- or long-term. We also discuss the variety of intervention strategies that have been suggested for divorcing families.

Mental Health

Psychopathology is often defined as a problem that could be classified according to the *Diagnostic and Statistical Manual of Mental Disorders* (American Psychiatric Association, 1987). It can also be described as the presence of maladaptive behavior and/or subjective distress. Internalizing problems refer to those areas of distress that are primarily within the person and do not so clearly involve external behaviors that bother other people. We expect that those involved in divorce will feel sad and often anxious for a period of time. We would be primarily concerned if there were long-term problems with anxiety, depression, or self-esteem.

The research in this area is subject to the same interpretative problems as in other areas. We need information as to the length of time since the divorce, as well as other events in the person's life. In addition, the scales designed to measure internalized problems are less reliable than those designed to measure externalized behavioral difficulties (Achenbach, McConaughy, & Howell, 1987). It is often adults who are asked to do ratings of children, and they may not be as aware of internalized problems. For example, Wallerstein and Kelly (1980) reported that parents were often unaware of the emotional distress of their children. It may be that parents are particularly likely to have difficulty with such awareness following divorce because they are themselves in distress and therefore not as sensitive to the problems of others, or because they would be made even more anxious if they were to acknowledge their children's distress. Finally, the children themselves may be protecting their parents by not letting them find out about their distress. For any one or all of these reasons, we would expect that the research on long-term internalization would be more complicated than that on externalized behavioral problems.

Some of the research in this area depends upon a clinical judgment of the child's level of adjustment. Abrams (1988) gave descriptions of the parents' relationship and a child case history to clinicians who were to make judgments about adjustment and treatment issues. Clinicians who had themselves experienced marital dissolution were more inclined to attribute healthy psychological adjustment and less need for treatment for children described as having experienced divorce two years in the past. Is this because clinicians with this experience are more accurate? Conversely, is it because they are unconsciously motivated to deny adverse effects of parental divorce?

We should also note that internalizing difficulties are more commonly found among girls than boys (e.g., Achenbach, Howell, Quay, & Conners, 1991). Those researchers who have not considered sex differences may have misleading results. This conclusion is supported by a meta-analysis of 50 studies of psychological adjustment in children in which depression, anxiety, or general happiness was measured. The studies for males only did not show a significant overall effect. Those studies that included both sexes or females only were statistically significant. This analysis also determined that overall effects were significant only for elementary- and high school-aged samples (Amato & Keith, 1991a). Their analysis of studies with adult, post-college samples included a category of psychological adjustment that combined depression, anxiety, and life satisfaction. There were no sex differences here although there were great differences associated with the source of the sample. Again, those samples obtained from a population seeking clinical help yielded much greater differences between the offspring of divorce and others when compared to samples obtained from other sources.

Research concerned specifically with depression and anxiety can demonstrate how such research can be more useful than merely giving information about incidence.

Depression

The term *depression* may refer to a temporary state or to a clinical syndrome that persists over time and a variety of situations. We are not concerned with the likelihood that depression will occur during the original process of adaptation, but rather whether there is a long-lasting problem. McDermott (1968) suggested, on the basis of clinical experience, that many children are clinically depressed following parental divorce. Wallerstein also reported high rates of depression among her sample; again it is difficult to determine what this conclusion means. Although her data were based on clinical interviews, Wallerstein did not necessarily give diagnoses of clinical depression. The interpretation of her conclusion is also complicated by the fact that there was no comparison group to determine a base rate of depression.

Although epidemiologic research sometimes indicates that risk for depression is related to a history of parental separation (e.g., Kendler, Neale, Kessler, Heath, & Eaves, 1992), the results of research comparing groups who have or have not experienced parental divorce are inconsistent; thus, we should not presently conclude that parental divorce necessarily increases the likelihood of clinical depression. A recent study by Fendrich, Warner, and Weissman (1990) found that parental depression was a better predictor of childhood depression than were family risk factors, which included both divorce and parental discord. However, they also suggested that parental divorce might be related to more debilitating forms of depression in children already at high risk. That is, those children who have a depressed parent and who experience parental divorce may be especially at risk. This is consistent with the literature on parental death in childhood, which finds no clearcut or consistent effect in adulthood (Crook & Eliot, 1980; Tennant, Bebbington, & Hurry, 1980).

The effects following divorce or death can also be less severe than clinical depression, based on findings obtained in some national probability samples. Because they provide no information about the age at divorce or other associated circumstances, these samples, by their nature, allow us only to compare those who experienced parental divorce as children with those who did not. Data from 1957 and 1976 (Kulka & Weingarten, 1979) show no relation with adult depression but did find that grown adults whose parents had divorced were more likely to say that bad things frequently happened to them and that they found bad events difficult to handle. This overall effect was reduced when socioeconomic status was statistically controlled and remained primarily for males.

Glenn and Kramer (1985) compared adults who had experienced parental death or divorce during childhood with those who had lived with both parents. Adult adjustment for males was equally negatively affected by death and divorce. For females, only parental divorce affected later adjustment. These adults reported that they were less happy and less satisfied with their family, friends, and community. Although statistically significant, only a small proportion of the variation in responses to these adjustment items was explained by childhood family status.

Anxiety

As with depression, one would expect to find that children experience transient anxiety as they are adjusting to various aspects of a parental divorce. Again, the question of concern here is whether or not there are anxiety disorders indicating an unusually high level of anxiety persisting over time and a variety of situations.

Without using clinical diagnoses, Hetherington (1988) has reported that six years after experiencing divorce, offspring were overrepresented in a cluster of youngsters described as lonely, unhappy, anxious, and insecure. However, these homes were also characterized by continued conflict or inappropriate parenting.

Emery (1982) reviewed some of the studies of anxiety disorders and phobias and found no consistent relation with family marital status. He did conclude that anxiety decreased with the passage of time and that parental conflict was a more salient predictor of anxiety. Fendrich et al. (1990) found that the diagnosis of anxiety disorders in several hundred children between the ages of 6 and 23 was not associated with any family risk factors, although parental depression did increase the likelihood of this disorder.

The 1957 and 1976 national surveys analyzed by Kulka and Weingarten (1979) found that adult offspring of divorce more often reported feeling high anxiety at times. They were also more likely to report that childhood had been the unhappiest time of their life.

Self-Concept or Self-Esteem

The terms *self-esteem* and *self-concept* refer to similar variables but are not synonymous. Self-concept generally refers to an overall perception of one's abilities or personality. Self-esteem most often refers to an emotional component or evaluation of one's worth. A meta-analysis (Amato & Keith, 1991b) of 34 studies of self-concept found that studies of children done after 1970 did not show an effect. Similarly, studies of adults from divorced families (Amato & Keith, 1991b) also did not reveal any negative effects upon self-concept. Of note, however, is that two studies in agreement with the general finding of no effect did relate lower self-concept to higher parental conflict, whether it occurred in divorced or married families (Raschke & Raschke, 1979; Slater & Haber, 1984).

The available empirical research suggests that parental divorce may be related to children's psychological adjustment in some contexts, although the relationship is weak and decreasing. Most of the research used in analyses that reached this conclusion was cross-sectional in nature. However, a recent longitudinal study of large national samples in both the United States and Great Britain (Cherlin, Furstenberg, Chase-Lansdale, Kiernan, Robins, Morrison, & Teitler, 1991) also supports the general view that effects are small and often associated with other variables. For this study, an adjustment scale was constructed from a variety of items, including a mixture of behaviors (e.g., disobedient at home or school) and feelings (e.g., sad or depressed; too fearful). Although boys whose parents had divorced between the beginning and end of the study had higher problem scores on the average, the effect of divorce was not significant when the amount of marital conflict in the home and the presence of problems prior to the divorce were taken into consideration.

We conclude that for externalizing and internalizing problems, divorce per se does not necessarily produce long-term problems. However, it is clear that the population of divorcing adults and divorced families may well be at risk because of other variables that often accompany divorce.

Social Functioning

Using data from the *National Longitudinal Study of Youth,* Hawkins and Eggebeen (1991) found no relation between the presence or absence of males in the home and social functioning among preschoolers when mothers were used as informants. The meta-analysis for data with children (Amato & Keith, 1991a) also found no relation between social adjustment and parental divorce when the data were obtained from a parent. However, significant differences occurred when the informant was the child or a teacher, or when observations were made by an outside researcher. The effects were larger for males than females. Their meta-analysis for adults (Amato & Keith, 1991b) found lower levels of social well-being for offspring of divorce. However, this effect was extremely small and when analyzed separately by sex, was present for females only.

Additional work in this area should take into consideration not only how the variable is assessed but also the specific nature of the behavior measured.

Eating Disorders

Clinical studies suggest an association between eating disorders and parental divorce (e.g., Robinson & Andersen, 1985). Holden and Robinson (1988) compared patients with either anorexia or bulimia with a control group and found that there was more parental divorce or separation in the group with an eating disorder. However, the groups also differed in race and social class. Three studies have been concerned with bulimia, in which individuals engage in binge eating and then force themselves to vomit. Igoin-Apfelbaum (1985) reported that a large proportion of bulimic women consulting a clinic were offspring of divorce and that this was considerably higher than the proportion for obese patients (Igoin-Apfelbaum & Apfelbaum, 1990). Notably, these parental divorces were so problematic that most of these patients could not maintain relationships with both parents. Dolan, Lieberman, Evans, and Lacey (1990) compared bulimic females and controls and found that, although there was a similar divorce rate, the bulimics reported greater parental conflict.

As in other areas, any relationship between parental divorce and eating disorders may be mediated by parental conflict. This does not mean that divorce or parent conflict are the only factors involved in an eating disorder, however. Fichter and Noegel (1990), for example, found evidence for a genetic component. What is more likely is that if there is some predisposition toward eating disorders, either on the basis of genetics or prior learning, the stresses associated with divorce may increase the probability of these symptoms.

■ _____

Life Story

Charlotte

Charlotte is a 19-year-old resident of Ohio, the daughter of an anesthesiologist and a nurse. Her parents, Gary and Carol, met at a party where Gary and some of his buddies from Harvard Medical School were getting "stoned." They soon married and while Gary was finishing his internship, Charlotte was born. Siblings Gail and Amanda were born one and three years later. The couple lived in eight different communities in the first nine years of marriage, with Charlotte making several moves in elementary school. These moves resulted not only from job changes but from the parents' relocating to more and more prestigious communities, with beautiful houses and beautiful people, characteristics important to Charlotte and her family. It was during elementary school that Charlotte remembers being awakened at night by hearing her parents fighting, often over her father's drinking. Although the parental fighting intensified over the next years, Gary became greatly involved with his children. He attended all of their extracurricular activities including swimming meets and band recitals, helped them with their homework, and went with them to meetings of Indian Princesses (an organization similar to Girl Scouts). Charlotte was never close to her mother, who seemed to suffer from mood swings and who, when angry at Charlotte, told her that she was just like her father. When Charlotte was a freshman in high school, her father moved out, supposedly temporarily, and both parents separately entered counseling. This ended within a month, and Gary filed for divorce. When he announced this to the family, a two-hour fight ensued, at which the children were present. They saw their father choking their mother and trying to hit her on the head with a hammer; they heard their mother screaming that she was going to kill herself and saw her swallowing antidepressants. Since that day, Carol and Gary have never talked to one another. Carol and the girls then learned that Gary had met and quickly become seriously involved with another woman. When his daughters found out about this, they were devastated; Charlotte remembers her father telling them that the other woman, Terry, had "great boobs"; with the encouragement of their mother, the girls stopped talking to Gary for almost one year.

Carol, who had not been working, took a part-time job, as did Charlotte. Primarily, though, the family was dependent upon money voluntarily given by Gary. One month when no money arrived, Carol pawned their musical instruments. She also asked Charlotte to see her father again with the hope that he might begin to send money. Gary took Charlotte to dinner and bought several outfits for her, but did not send money. Carol was furious at Charlotte and told her that she was selfish. The family began to disintegrate. Carol often left the children, who were from 11 to 14 years old. They fed themselves and the pets and did their own laundry, rarely talking to one another. They now had to ask their friends for rides to band and swim practice, or not get there. Finally, Charlotte came home to find her mother unconscious from a deliberate overdose of pills. After this, when she was in school, Charlotte worried about whether her mother would be alive when she arrived home. Her grades dropped to Cs. Occasionally she took her mother's Xanax herself with the intention not of killing herself, but of getting some rest. Although Charlotte took on the responsibility of caring for her mother, the relationship was still a tumultuous one. Her mother met and rapidly became engaged to Paul, who borrowed money from Carol to pay off thousands of dollars of debts. Charlotte called her father and went to live with him. She did not attend the wedding or speak to her mother for half a year. Her father sent Charlotte to a psychiatrist who diagnosed her as depressed; when he additionally suggested that the rest of the family also had major problems, Gary decided that Charlotte no longer needed help. Unfortunately, while at her father's, she kept a diary in which she noted her negative feelings about her stepmother and stepsiblings. Terry found and showed this to Charlotte's father. Gary "disowned" Charlotte just as she was to leave for college. Because of a legal agreement, however, her financial support for college was never in question.

Charlotte went to college out of state, and was diagnosed as bulimic in her freshman year. This symptom ceased when she and her father again began to talk. In the next few years, Charlotte achieved a rapprochement with both of her parents, largely by ignoring what everyone had said and done in the past. She still does not like Paul, who has never worked since marrying her mother. Charlotte believes that the relationship with her father will never be the same as it was prior to the separation and feels that Gary is closer to his stepchildren than to his own children. She is also aware that, although Gary is a successful physician, he has never gone a day without having several drinks. Although Gary still refers to Carol as "the witch," Charlotte believes that her parents would have worked out their relationship if her father had not met Terry. She attempts to get along with Terry, but still resents that Terry tried to tell Charlotte how psychologically "crazy" her mother was.

Presently, Charlotte is in a premed curriculum, earning higher grades than she received in high school. Charlotte is exceptionally attractive and well-dressed. Living in a sorority, she is socially skilled in interactions with both males and females. However, Charlotte is aware that she is not really close to people. Generally, she does not trust others and deliberately chooses to be dependent upon no one now or in the future. Only after it is clear that her career is set does Charlotte wish to begin thinking about marriage.

Physical Health

Offspring in one-parent families have more health problems and are more likely to use health services than those in two-parent families (Cafferata & Kasper, 1985; Jennings & Sheldon, 1985; Moreno, 1989; Worobey, Angel, & Worobey, 1988). Guidubaldi and Cleminshaw (1985) found that all members of divorced families, parents and children, had on the average poorer physical health as compared to a matched sample of still married families. Amato and Keith (1991b) located 11 studies that considered the physical health or disability of adults who had experienced parental divorce. As compared to those from non-divorced families, offspring of divorce were slightly less healthy. These physical problems could be stress-related. However, other interpretations are possible. For example, health practices and the use of medical resources clearly differ between social classes. Unless studies control for the social class of participants, one cannot conclude that parental divorce results in a greater likelihood of long-term health problems.

Interventions with Divorcing Families

Offspring of divorce are overrepresented among those referred for therapy or counseling. The *National Survey of Children,* an assessment of a representative national sample in 1976, found that 13 percent of the children from divorced households had seen a psychologist or psychiatrist at some time, whereas among those in married families, 5.5 percent had

(Zill, 1978). Not surprisingly, children whose parents request counseling are not like the "average" child of divorce in that those in counseling are more likely to show behavioral and social competence problems (Isaacs, Leon, & Donohue, 1986). As previously indicated, even those children who are not manifesting problems will be dealing with some emotional and cognitive adjustment issues.

Intervention programs can be preventive or may be designed specifically for those already having difficulty. However, of the available programs, few have been emperically evaluated for effectiveness (Grych & Fincham, 1992). Stolberg and Cullen (1983) have suggested that preventive programs should hasten the adjustment period and prevent such things as aggression, inappropriate school behavior and performance, and psychological disorders. Divorce mediation can be conceptualized as a preventive program.

Among divorcing or divorced parents, high levels of parent stress or symptomology are associated with a greater number of child symptoms that do not decrease with time (Woody, Colley, Schlegelmilch, Maginn, & Balsanek, 1984). This suggests that any procedure that results in better functioning of the adults is likely to help the offspring. Unfortunately, this hypothesis has not been tested empirically.

In contrast to individual therapy, self-help groups may be desirable because they are typically less expensive and provide a wider range of psychological support. A study of the effects of intervention groups for recently separated adults (Bloom, Hodges, & Caldwell, 1982) asked participants to attend a session on one of five topics. These included employment problems; legal and financial issues; parenting concerns; housing and homemaking arrangements; and social and emotional well-being. All groups reported less anxiety and better physical well-being as compared to a control group. Some positive effects were still evident four years later (Bloom, Hodges, Kern, & McFaddin, 1985).

Some groups for separated or divorced parents focus on overall adjustment (e.g., Addington, 1992; Haffey & Cohen, 1992), whereas others emphasize the parenting aspects of post-divorce life. Warren and Amara (1985) found that parents with greater stress benefit the most from such a group. In addition, parents expressed more satisfaction with educational groups than with those that are primarily for emotional support.

When there are clear-cut problems on the part of children, parents often decide that children need individual or group counseling. A number of preventive group programs designed for children are available (e.g., Bonkowski, Bequette, & Boomhower, 1984; Ciborowski, 1984; Gendler, 1986; Hammond, 1981; Kaminsky, 1986; Morganett, 1990).

The majority of these have been devised for use in schools. However, there are programs for those younger and older (e.g., Rossiter, 1988), as well as programs for "adult children" of divorce (e.g., Fassell, 1991).

Garvin, Leber, and Kalter (1991) have described a program, the Family Styles Project, devised for elementary school children whose parents are divorcing. The ten weekly sessions have two adult coleaders and specified goals, including normalizing the experience of divorce; clarifying issues such as custody and visitation; providing a forum to talk about difficult feelings; helping children develop strategies for coping; and sharing with parents the concerns that occupy offspring. A six-month follow-up comparing those who had been in the program with children on the waiting list found positive changes.

School counselors usually work in groups with offspring of divorce (e.g., Pfeifer & Abrams, 1984). These programs are preventive, as they are carried out with all children and not just those having unusual problems with divorce (cf. Cowen, Hightower, Pedro-Carroll, & Work, 1989). Such programs can be beneficial to participating students (Alpert-Gillis, Pedro-Carroll, & Cowen, 1989; Gwynn & Brantley, 1987; Jupp & Purcell, 1992; Pedro-Carroll & Cowen, 1985; Pedro-Carroll, Cowen, Hightower, & Guare, 1986).

Programs for children can also involve parents in various ways. In a unique approach, Bonkowski, Boomhower, and Bequette (1985) analyzed letters written to divorcing parents by children and found that the content differed depending upon the sex of the child, with boys angrier and girls more anxious. Many themes were identified, including questions that the children wanted answered. The Divorce Adjustment Project (Stolberg & Mahler, 1989) uses concurrent programs for children and single parents, as do a number of other programs (e.g., Epstein, Borduin, & Wexler, 1985; McLeod & Vonk, 1992; Williams, Wright, & Rosenthal, 1983).

Only one study has compared the use of support groups for children alone, support groups for the parents alone, and a group for parents and children. Offspring improved most in self-concept in the children-alone group. Parents in the parents-alone group improved most in adjustment. Improvements were maintained at a five-month follow-up (Stolberg & Garrison, 1985).

In addition to parents, Nichols (1985) suggested involving grandparents. Gurman, Kniskern, and Pinsof (1986) noted, in a review of research on family therapy, that although it is widely believed that involving all of the members of the family is most desirable for divorced families, there is no empirical support for this conclusion.

Newly forming stepfamilies would seem especially to profit from family therapy. The particular issues to be dealt with appear to be different from those that arise with the original divorce. The relationship with the former spouse is likely to need renegotiation (Ahrons & Perlmutter, 1982). In addition, the children have to accept the solidity of the new marriage and learn to deal with the stepparent as an authority (Cissna, Cox, & Bochner, 1990). Other issues include the need for new roles and the possibility of competition and rivalry among stepsiblings (Mills, 1984). Of course, therapy is not the only way in which help may be available for stepfamilies. Support groups (e.g., Brady & Ambler, 1982) have also been suggested.

In addition to self-help groups, a variety of self-help books is available (e.g., Kalter, 1990; Lansky, 1991). There are no data regarding how many people use such resources following divorce. Furthermore, even when such books give appropriate advice, it may not be accurately interpreted and applied (Christensen, Johnson, Phillips, & Glasgow, 1980). As a result, group and individual training approaches may be superior to the use of written materials alone.

Bibliotherapy (Pardeck, 1989) can also be used as an adjunct to other therapies. Appropriate books for children necessarily differ according to developmental level. Pardeck and Pardeck (1985) suggested that counselors should use books about divorce that hold out realistic hopes, do not blame any one character for the divorce, focus on everyday life following divorce, and mention ways in which a character has made adjustments. Available children's fiction in our local libraries mainly featured white and upper-middle-class families with about one third of the children living with their father. Themes included children adjusting to a parent dating, the mother getting a job, financial problems, moves, additional responsibilities, and stepfamilies.

A variety of media, including cassette tapes (Kenny & Black, undated), films, filmstrips, videotapes (see Kimmons & Gaston, 1986), and a newsletter for single mothers and fathers (Nelson, 1986) are available. Among the more unusual materials is a board game entitled *The Divorce Game,* which is intended to be used by a small group of children with an adult leader (Theodore, 1990).

Evaluative studies comparing intervention strategies are rare (Grych & Fincham, 1992). One research study compared participant ratings of the use of bibliotherapy, structured group counseling, and individual counseling. Participants were early adolescents whose families were changing for any of a number of reasons, including divorce. Both bibliotherapy and group counseling were rated as more helpful than individual counseling, although there were no differences in actual outcomes (Sheridan, Baker, & de-Lissovoy, 1984). This suggests that in many cases, relatively inexpensive educational programs may be as useful as the more costly individual counseling.

Because of the wide variation both in individual reactions to stress and in the specific divorce situation, it is unlikely that any one approach will be appropriate for every family. However, people working with divorcing families need to focus on the positive results of this experience (Hutchinson & Spangler-Hirsch, 1989).

Overview

The expectation that divorce will have a negative effect upon offspring has, of course, influenced the variables that research has assessed. The research reviewed in this chapter suggests small average differences in mental health-related variables between offspring of divorce and those who have not experienced divorce. However, few of these studies consider whether the behavior of the offspring of divorce falls within the "normal" or "healthy" range.

Furthermore, any positive effects will be difficult to locate until our research approach has changed. Levin (1989) concluded, after examining data from nationally representative surveys, that the impact of marital adjustment is small and generally indirect (that is, influenced by such variables as conflict or economic difficulty). He further suggested that where differences were found, they were about as likely to improve the development of the child from the divorced household as to retard it. However, it is not clear whether these are long-term consequences or refer to such changes as life being improved by the absence of an abusing or alcoholic parent.

For all of us, life presents stress and requires adjustment. It is not possible and probably not even desirable that we should try to protect children from all stresses. As Bandura (1989) has noted,

> Development of resilient self-efficacy requires some experience in mastering difficulties through perseverant effort. If people experience only easy successes, they come to expect quick results and their sense of efficacy is easily undermined by failure. Some setbacks and difficulties in human pursuits serve a useful purpose in teaching that success usually requires sustained effort. After people become convinced they have what it takes to succeed, they persevere in the face of adversity and quickly rebound from setbacks. By sticking it out through tough times, they emerge from adversity with a stronger sense of efficacy. (p. 1179)

Adequate socialization requires that we teach children how to deal with change and loss as well as other unpleasant life happenings. Unfortunately, all of the people involved when a marriage ends are likely to be experiencing distress; parents as well as children may benefit from deliberate educational and therapeutic experiences.

Summary

- Long-term effects of parental divorce are less apparent now than in the past.
- Most offspring of divorce will not display behavior problems or symptoms of psychopathology or maladjustment. However, the stresses related to parental divorce may exacerbate problems that already exist.
- The relation between parental divorce and an offspring's adjustment is probably mediated by numerous variables, including parental psychopathology and conflict.
- The adjustment of both parents and children can be hastened by participation in any of a variety of deliberate intervention procedures.

10

Implications and Recommendations

Preview

In this final chapter, we tie together the themes discussed throughout this book. We consider issues relevant to numerous specific outcome variables, including the implications of this research for social policy and for future research.

The Effects of Divorce

The data described thus far show clearly that offspring of divorced and never-divorced parents differ in a variety of ways, but that most of these average differences are not large. In fact, in some content areas, although statistically significant, the differences are trivial. Furthermore, the differences between these groups appear to be less prominent now than in the 1950s and 1960s, the methodologically more sophisticated studies show smaller differences (Amato & Keith, 1991a), and differences within groups of offspring of divorce are larger than differences between offspring of divorced and non-divorced parents (Barber & Eccles, 1992). Parental divorce, then, does not necessarily put a child at risk; knowing that a child is from a single-mother family is a poor predictor of the child's current or future functioning.

Levin (1989) concluded from nationally representative surveys that the impact of marital adjustment is small and generally indirect. He also suggested that where differences are found, they are about as likely to improve the development of the child from the divorced household as to retard it. For example, the departure from the traditional masculine and feminine stereotypes exhibited by some offspring of divorce can be viewed as positive and beneficial (Parke, 1981). Similarly, Weiss (1979) suggested that the single-parent family may require children to behave more responsibly and to be treated as full-functioning members so that children develop self-esteem, independence, and a sense of competence. Few other possible benefits have been investigated (Barber & Eccles, 1992).

Equally clear is that children of divorce are not a homogeneous group and that they do not react to parental divorce in the same way. It is popularly believed that boys are more affected than girls by parental divorce. Meta-analyses of the relevant literature investigating children's cognitive performance (Salzman, 1987) and children's adjustment (Love-Clark, 1984) support this contention. Brooks-Gunn and Furstenberg (1986) found this to be true for offspring of adolescent mothers (many of whom are also single). Hetherington (1989) made this finding one of the major points in her presidential address to the Society for Research on Child Development.

Although it is reasonable to conclude that boys and girls may react differently, we are reluctant to make a judgment concerning who is more affected, in part because girls' experiences in single-parent families have not been examined extensively. For example, Kalter et al. (1985) have suggested that female offspring's heterosexual relationships and feminine self-esteem are more likely to be affected. Furthermore, Wallerstein's case studies suggest that effects may not be apparent until girls enter young adulthood, yet most of the extant research concerns children. Finally, Zaslow (1988, 1989) reviewed 27 studies that examined sex differences and found that more than a third depart from the predicted pattern of more negative consequences for boys.

In addition to sex differences, reactions to single-parenting differ by race (e.g., Stevenson & Black, 1988). Unfortunately, these differences are again difficult to interpret, due to lack of data. However, the literature on adult adjustment to the role of single parent shows that African Americans may cope more successfully than Caucasians (Fine & Schwebel, 1987). As a result, the single-parent experience may lead to different child outcomes in African-American and Caucasian families. The extent to which we can generalize on this point is unclear, because we know essentially nothing about these processes in other racial groups.

Age also appears to make a difference. Unfortunately, the evidence is contradictory. Some suggest that older children are more affected (e.g., Wallerstein & Kelly, 1980), whereas others indicate that younger children are more affected (e.g., Allison & Furstenberg, 1989).

Children of different ages differ in their level of cognitive development, and limited intellectual functioning can lead to adjustment difficulties. For example, an insightful 3-year-old boy whose divorced parents were in litigation for several years and who were still having problems resolving questions of visitation, made the following comment when told that it was all right to love both his parents. "But when I'm with my Mommy I don't like my Daddy and when I'm with my Daddy I think my Mommy is dumb" (author's files).

In addition to its impact on intellectual understanding, age can also affect the possible behaviors that researchers measure, whether these behaviors show distress or coping. Infants may cry and show sleeping and eating disorders as a reaction to trauma, whereas adolescents may exhibit scholastic difficulties or deviant behaviors (Beverina, 1989).

The problem with making generalizations about age is that dependent variables are defined differently across age groups. Additionally the child's age is confounded with the length of time spent in a single-parent home and the length of time since the disruption occurred. Although we believe that age makes a difference, it is unlikely that we can predict or analyze differences in a simple, straightforward way.

Explaining the Differences

There are at least three distinct explanations that are not mutually exclusive for the differences between offspring of divorced and of never-divorced families. They are interrelated and difficult to distinguish empirically. Each suggests that divorce, per se, is related only indirectly to child outcomes.

The traditional explanation is father absence. Children of divorced mothers do not have resident fathers to look to as role models, sources of emotional support, and practical help and supervision (Amato & Keith, 1991a). In addition, stress can result from a father's absence and a mother's inability to compensate (e.g., Colletta, 1983). This implies that stress is the real culprit, and that father's absence has only an indirect effect.

A second explanation attributes the differences between offspring of divorced and never-divorced parents to various forms of family dysfunction, including conflict between parents and difficulty with the transition from a two-parent to a one-parent family. One could argue that dysfunctional families are more likely to divorce so that in addition to the divorce, these children are more likely to have experienced various forms of family dysfunction than children who have not experienced divorce (Cherlin et al., 1991). This viewpoint emphasizes parental values, childrearing practices, lower parental attachment, less supervision, more favorable attitudes toward divorce, greater stress, and problematic parent-child relations (McLanahan & Booth, 1989).

The third explanation, economic deprivation, suggests that divorce results in economic hardship and is associated with working more hours, less parental supervision, lower parenting skills, greater likelihood of children dropping out of school (McLanahan & Booth, 1989), and family violence (Gelles, 1989). Decreased income can also cause mother-only families to live in economically and socially isolated neighborhoods, which lowers opportunities for economic mobility and raises the likelihood both of dropping out of school and of offspring becoming teen parents (McLanahan & Booth, 1989). These neighborhoods also provide fewer safe places for children to play (Colletta, 1983).

Again, it seems unlikely that absence of a father as a role model has a direct impact on offspring. Much of what is typically attributed to divorce is probably due to aspects of family functioning that were present before the divorce (Cherlin et al., 1991). In particular, parental conflict is known to harm children's development and is clearly related to parental divorce (Emery, et al., 1984; Amato & Keith, 1991a).

Although parental conflict is likely to be the most important variable, economic hardship is also important. In a meta-analysis, Amato and Keith (1991b) showed adults who had experienced parental divorce as children obtained less education, had a lower material quality of life, and were in occupations that offered less prestige and less satisfaction than offspring of never-divorced parents (Amato & Keith, 1991b). Furthermore, economics are probably more important than family structure in that when the divorced mother's income is low, stress is high. This in turn is related to poorer child-rearing practices (Colletta, 1983).

Implications for Social Policy

An increase in single-mother families can be viewed as social progress as it marks women's ability to survive economically outside of marriage. Conversely, it can also be viewed as problematic, as when African-American men leave families that they cannot support financially (McLanahan & Booth, 1989). In one respect, both positions are wrong in that each ignores the social class issues that the other addresses. However, regardless of how single-mother families are viewed, many children are being raised in them. A responsible society will provide families, regardless of their structure, the opportunity to care for their children. As Ahlberg and DeVita (1992) suggest,

> Valuing the family should not be confused with valuing a particular family form. . . . Social legislation (or "pro-family" policies) narrowly designed to reinforce only one model of the American family is likely to be shortsighted and have the unintended consequence of weakening, rather than strengthening, family ties. (pg. 39)

Social policy makers may have the largest impact on the legal process of divorce. However, in reality only about 10 percent of divorcing couples end up in court. Most dissolutions are worked out between lawyers. As a result, members of the legal profession, members of divorcing families, and social policy makers need accurate information and an understanding of the processes producing that information. So-called "experts" continue to use untested assumptions and unsubstantiated generalizations (e.g., that divorce affects boys more than girls, that sex-typed behavior is necessary, and that parental role models are essential) to guide their recommendations (e.g., Miller, 1986).

If our goal is to decrease conflict and increase economic well-being, to what should the legal system work? The options include reconciliation (as suggested by "traditional values"), punishing the guilty, an equal split, the best interest of the child, and that which is fairest to everyone. The current choice is typically the best interest of the child. But what is in the child's best interest? Sole custody? Joint custody? Strict visitation? Should the custodial parent have strict control? Should visitation be contingent upon child support? What are the rights of grandparents?

As we have seen, answers to these questions are far from simple, and divorcing families differ in a variety of ways. Clearly, we cannot institute the same solution for every family. For example, some experts recommend joint custody as a mandatory policy. Although joint legal custody should be an available option and serves as a symbol to fathers that they have rights and obligations (Furstenberg & Cherlin, 1991), it is not always a viable solution. Some jurisdictions (e.g., Atlanta, GA and

Indianapolis, IN) now require divorcing parents with children to attend educational or counseling programs, but the efficacy of such programs has not been evaluated.

Although there are no simple answers, the best interests of the children are furthered by helping parents function as parents regardless of the particular family structure. We have no culturally shared positive image of how custodial or noncustodial single parents should behave. Early intervention will help those involved understand that they can continue to be a family even when the family structure does not match the traditional ideal. Boss (1986) suggested that a family will become pathological if one of its members is not interacting as the rest of the family perceives it should. However, legislation that pushes dysfunctional families to stay together, such as making divorce more difficult or impossible, will not create well-functioning families (Furstenberg & Cherlin, 1991).

Policies that encourage early intervention from informed lawyers, mental health professionals, or family life educators may encourage optimal family functioning and decrease conflict. Counselors might educate teachers about the effects of divorce (cf., Cantrell, 1986; Cook & McBride, 1982). Schools could address divorce and family life in existing courses, and could routinely send report cards or announcements of parent activities to noncustodial as well as to custodial parents.

A primary problem with the current legal system is that it is adversarial. Even informed legal professionals find it difficult to encourage cooperation and compromise while fully representing the interests of their clients. Gardner (1989) has suggested that child custody decisions should be entirely removed from courtroom litigation.

Mediation is a reasonable alternative (e.g., Saayman & Saayman, 1988–1989) and some clients, particularly fathers, actually prefer mediation to adversarial procedures (Emery & Wyer, 1987; Kruk, 1992). In mediation, a couple works with a single consultant who facilitates agreement on disputed issues. The research literature has demonstrated that, compared to using the typical approach, couples are more satisfied with mediation and are less likely to go back to court (Sprenkle & Storm, 1983). Mediation can also influence child outcomes. In one study, children whose parents went through mediation were less likely to develop delinquent behaviors than were those who had gone through a contested divorce (Stull & Kaplan, 1987).

The use of mediation, either by state or court mandate, appears to be increasing, although it is unclear whether this is an attempt to relieve the court system or because of a belief that it is better for the participants. Clearly, mediation does not work in all cases. In addition, we do not know whether post-divorce adjustment differs between couples who choose mediation voluntarily and those where mediation was court-ordered.

Besides addressing legal issues, responsible social policy must also consider the economic well-being of single-mother families. Single-mother families have higher poverty rates than do other families. Single mothers bear most of the economic costs of rearing children, even though their earning capacity is limited by lack of work experience, sex discrimination, and the high cost of child care (McLanahan & Booth, 1989).

Enhancing the economic well-being of single-mother families can be achieved through a variety of steps: changing mothers' ability to earn, assuring that income support is paid by noncustodial parents, and in some instances, providing temporary government subsidies (McLanahan & Booth, 1989; Furstenberg & Cherlin, 1991). Increasing mothers' earnings can be accomplished through a variety of mechanisms aimed at changing the employment opportunities of women in general. This includes equal pay for equal work and comparable worth. Policies should be designed to provide assistance with reentry into the work force, to retool unskilled workers, to provide job supports, and to recognize the family responsibilities of all employees, including mothers and fathers (Pleck, 1990; Sampson, 1987). Interestingly, these approaches would benefit most families, not just those who experience divorce.

Increasing child support payments by noncustodial parents is not unreasonable, if such increases do not push the noncustodial parent (and his or her new family) into poverty as well. In 1990, only about half of women who were awarded child support actually received full payments (Ahlburg & DeVita, 1992). Typically fixed amounts that do not fluctuate with earnings or with the cost of living, legal support payments do not reflect the real cost of child rearing. In 1990 the average amount of child support actually received by mothers was just under $3,000 (Ahlburg & DeVita, 1992). Furthermore, increased financial responsibility should also be coupled with increased parental rights concerning how the children should be raised and how the money is to be spent. Currently, this is not the case in sole-custody families.

To help ensure the continuation of support payments, a variety of mechanisms have been suggested. These include making visitation contingent upon support payments and increasing the availability of enforcement options (e.g., automatic wage assignments; incarceration; self-starting collection systems). Interestingly, fathers who pay some support (regardless of the amount) are more likely to see their children regularly (Furstenberg, Peterson, Nord, & Zill, 1983). However, we do not know if more coercive methods of enforcing payment of support would attenuate this relationship.

Finally, any government intervention should be temporary and designed to increase women's independence and ability to earn, but not to foster continued dependence on the state or increased numbers of children. Policies should not reward or punish "traditional" families, but should encourage economic well-being among both women and men, so that women can choose to enter marriages freely rather than for economic stability. Australia's program to provide single mothers access to higher education has proven successful in preparing them for careers, as well as in increasing the educational aspirations of their offspring (Burns, 1992).

Staying Together for the Sake of the Children

Popular culture clings to the myth that the only way to rear happy, healthy children is in a traditional two-parent home. This myth suggests that children of divorce are permanently devastated and must have a model of a working marriage at home in order to have one themselves (e.g., Kantrowitz, 1992). For example, Dr. Edward Beal was quoted in *Newsweek* as saying that offspring of divorce "look into the future through the filter of potential divorce" (Kantrowitz, 1992, p. 49). Although this may be true, it can be interpreted, perhaps more appropriately, that offspring of divorce do not look at marriage through rose-colored glasses or harbor unrealistic expectations about married life. Furthermore, claims that offspring of divorce are uniformly devastated simply are unsubstantiated by the bulk of the evidence presented here— particularly that of the methodologically sophisticated large-scale and longitudinal studies.

Conservative social critics (e.g., Collier, 1991) imply that single-parent families will eventually lead to the downfall of American culture. They misinterpret research findings as consistent with the deficit model and erroneously suggest, "It is *not* better to divorce than to raise children in a home with tension and bickering" (p. 249). In contrast, some social scientists suggest that even a father's psychological absence from the home may cause more disequilibrium than his total absence, because total absence would at least permit reorganization of the family system where roles could be reassigned to the active members (Boss, 1986).

Research findings clearly show that unhappy or conflict-ridden two-parent homes are more deleterious to family members than are stable single-parent homes. An inaccessible, rejecting, or hostile parent in a nuclear family is more detrimental than an absent parent. Children from divorced or two-parent homes who experience interparental conflict or parental marital unhappiness are at greater risk than children from one- or two-parent homes that are relatively harmonious or happy (Booth & Edwards, 1989; Emery, 1982; Pietropinto, 1985; Stoneman, Brody, & Burke, 1989; Webster-Stratton & Hammond, 1990).

In some cases, divorce may be a positive solution to destructive family functioning if the divorce reduces or eliminates the conflict and hostility (Barber & Eccles, 1992). In addition, a good relationship with one parent can mediate a bad relationship with the other. Furthermore, an offspring's perceptions regarding the quality of the father-child relationship is a better predictor of adjustment than either the amount of conflict in the home or the family structure (Stevenson, 1990).

A cross-cultural perspective suggests that idealizing the two-parent family as the only way (or the only right way) to rear children may be peculiar to Western thought. Surbey (1990) suggested,

> The classical findings on father absence are based on western cultures where it is the norm for children to be raised by both parents and have led to the somewhat biased expectation that loss of a male role model leads to defects in sex-role [sic] formation and behavior. However, in some cultures, it is customary for fathers to have little or only indirect input in childraising. Paternal investment varies both within and across cultures and the expectation of psychological deficits in father-absent children may reflect the ethnocentrism of western psychologists. It is unlikely that [natural] selection would have created an ontogeny so fragile that it could result in whole populations of children exhibiting "psychological deficits." It is much more likely that children have evolved appropriate mechanisms which permit the development of competency in a number of different environmental conditions (pg. 17).

The Future of the American Family

It has long been suggested that the American family is in trouble (Furstenberg et al., 1983). Only one in five families fits the image of a sole-wage earner husband, a wife at home, and at least two minor children (Ahlburg & DeVita, 1992). Clearly, few families fit the definition of the much touted "traditional" family. Most mothers are now employed outside their homes, and most offspring live with just one parent at some time during their childhood. The rate of single-parenthood in the United States is the highest among western industrialized countries. However, the proportion of single-parent families has increased throughout the western world over the last two decades (Burns, 1992).

Attitudes about marriage and divorce have also changed over the last 40 years. In the United States, divorce became more socially acceptable during the 1960s and 1970s. Shortly thereafter, marriage apparently became less desirable, with more people marrying later or cohabitating (Burns, 1992).

Although laws concerning divorce have become less restrictive since the early 1970s, increased divorce rates were well underway before the legal changes. Therefore, the change in the law cannot be said to have caused the spread of divorce, but legislative changes do seem to have accounted for a shift to a higher divorce rate overall (Burns, 1992).

Given a broadened historical context, these changes in the family may be more apparent than real. Some argue that the average length of marriages has not changed much historically (e.g., Fisher, 1990; Skolnick, 1991). They imply that the idealized family of the 1950s was the historical exception rather than the rule. In the past, although divorce did not occur at such a high rate, family structure changed due to either abandonment or death. For example, less than half of the fathers in French peasant families of the seventeenth century were still alive at the marriage of their eldest sons (Bullough, 1990).

In June of 1991, the National Commission on Children (1991), chaired by Senator J. D. Rockefeller IV of Virginia, issued a 520-page report suggesting that, "Children do best when they have the personal involvement and material support of a father and a mother and when both parents fulfill their responsibility to be loving providers" (pg. 66). Although we agree that children benefit from the care of loving adults, the issue is whether this can happen when the parents are not living together.

Even after divorce, the majority of parents continue to feel an obligation and attachment to their children. Most remarry. Through their own marriages and children, the offspring of divorce are also committed to establishing a family. We suggest that rather than being in danger, the "family" continues to evolve, and our expectations about family functioning must also evolve.

Future Research Directions

Although we have learned a great deal about the differences between children in single- and two-parent families and have some ideas about the mechanisms causing these differences, many contested findings and unanswered questions remain.

There are no long-term studies analyzing the psychological effects of the major divorce-related economic issues (Wallerstein, 1991). What impact does the decline in family income and greater economic insecurity of the child have? What happens when the child reaches age 18 and support ends? How do significant economic discrepancies between the parents' households over the post-divorce years influence offspring?

Other unanswered questions concern child custody and visitation. Is there a short- or long-term difference for a 9-year-old boy that depends upon whether his mother or father is the custodial parent? Should one parent be given sole custody, or should a preference be given to joint custody? We do not have enough data on variations in custody arrangements to provide clear answers.

As discussed in chapter 4, we also need more research on the offspring's relationship with the nonresidential parent. Extant findings are inconsistent. Approximately one child in six sees a noncustodial father once a week. Over half see their father less than once a year (Furstenberg et al., 1983). More specifically, there are no long-term studies looking at patterns of overnight visiting for infants and toddlers (Wallerstein, 1991). We also need to know more about stepfathers; particularly when mothers remarry, noncustodial fathers have limited contact (Furstenberg et al., 1983).

Again, we need more data on ethnic and racial variations. Most research focuses on middle-class Caucasian families, so our data base needs to be expanded (Wallerstein, 1991). We do know that a larger proportion of African-American children experience single mothering and for longer periods of time (Furstenberg et al., 1983). The larger proportion of African-American families headed by single mothers is at least partially the result of a smaller proportion of employed African-American males (Sampson, 1987), making African-American family disruption a consequence, rather than a cause, of persistent poverty in the African-American community. Unfortunately, we know almost nothing about any other racial or ethnic group.

We also need to know more about how offsprings' developmental levels influence their adaptation to family transitions. Most of the extant research concerns children and adolescents, but many of the findings concerning age-related differences are confounded by the age of the child and the duration of single parenting. We know almost nothing about how infants are influenced by parental divorce, and we know even less about the reactions of adult offspring.

Whatever the question being considered, we need to recognize the historical shifts in the prevalence of divorce and the attitude changes that have accompanied these shifts. Public approval of marital dissolution increased dramatically between 1962 and 1980. Furthermore, those who have divorced are more likely to approve of it as an option; virtually all women who have been separated or divorced express approval later

(Thornton, 1985). How have these changes in attitudes influenced children of divorce? Do public attitudes toward divorce determine child-outcomes? Can we apply generalizations from data gathered during earlier decades to children who experience parental divorce today?

Although published research supports the use of intervention programs, we need more research, using multiple measures of outcome, that compares different types of interventions (Webster-Stratton & Hammond, 1990). Does it make a difference if there are co-leaders of both sexes in a group? Are groups more helpful in dealing with certain issues or at certain times in the divorce process? Would involving siblings increase program effectiveness? Are positive effects the result of a program's content, or does simply talking about the experience help? Research concerning cost-effectiveness and court-mandated brief programs is particularly lacking. All of this research should be sensitive to possible effects of the child's age, sex, and race.

Given the prediction that most children born in the 70s will not live with both biological parents throughout childhood (Furstenberg et al., 1983), we need to begin thinking of the "traditional" family as the exception rather than the norm or the ideal. Research that rests on the "deficit" model and assumes that the behavior of children in two-parent families represents the norm is misguided. We need to focus on how to help parents raise healthy children regardless of family structure.

In addition, we need to direct research toward helping children adapt to change, develop and maintain relationships, and end relationships. Furstenberg et al. (1983) reported that 37.3 percent of children reexperience disruption of their parents' marriage after entering a step-family. Nearly as many children have two or more major transitions as have one, and at least 1 in 10 will experience three or more parental marital transitions before they reach the age of 18.

Finally, we need to know if the apparent consequences of parental divorce and single mothering reflect preexisting conditions among couples who divorce, if troubled couples are more likely to break up and to have troubled children than happy couples, and if children from these marriages would have done poorly regardless of whether divorce had occurred (McLanahan & Booth, 1989). More longitudinal studies that begin before disruption occurs and last through multiple transitions would be particularly helpful.

Overview

The extant empirical literature leads us to question assumptions about the deleterious effects of parental divorce and single mothering. Certainly the ending of a marriage and changes in family configuration will cause pain and distress for those involved. Coping and adaptation will be required. To assume that parental divorce inevitably leads to adjustment difficulties in offspring, however, continues to propagate the myth that healthy, well-adjusted children can only be reared in families that include a parent of each gender, each playing a prescribed role. Such an assumption also ignores the growing body of literature suggesting that our definition of family must be transformed to focus on dynamic processes rather than on structure.

We must carefully consider our assumptions about family functioning, because these assumptions influence the way we design research, interpret findings, and apply those findings in the legal and mental health professions and in developing social policy. As Michael Rutter (1971) noted several years ago,

> We are still not sufficiently in the habit of critically examining the facts about a question before arriving at our conclusions about it. . . . Many of the statements I have quoted imply that we understand exactly what sort of upbringing a child needs and precisely which factors cause psychiatric disorder in children. But we do not, and it is our failure to *recognize* our ignorance which has led to these confident but contradictory claims. It is not the ignorance as such which is harmful but rather our "knowing" so many things that are not true. Our theories on the importance of the family have multiplied and become increasingly certain long before we know what are the facts the theories have to explain. (p. 234)

Summary

- The differences between offspring of divorced and non-divorced families are small.
- Offspring of divorce are not a homogeneous group.
- The differences between offspring whose parents have divorced and those who have not can be attributed to paternal absence, family dysfunction, and economic deprivation, rather than to divorce per se.
- Unhappy, conflict-ridden homes are more harmful to offspring than are stable single-parent homes.
- Social policy should encourage responsible parenting rather than favor one family structure over another.

- Rather than focus on the differences between offspring of divorce and others, future research should focus on family processes that influence child development.
- The American family continues to evolve.

REFERENCES

Abrams, T. (1988). The influence of family disruption on clinician bias in the assessment of children. *Journal of Divorce, 11,* 189–205.

Achenbach, T. M., Howell, C. T., Quay, H. C., & Conners, C. K. (1991). National survey of problems and competencies among four- to sixteen-year-olds: Parents' reports for normative and clinical samples. *Monographs of the Society for Research in Child Development, 56.*

Achenbach, T. M., McConaughy, S. H., & Howell, C. T. (1987). Child-adolescent behavioral and emotional problems: Implications of cross-informant correlations for situational specificity. *Psychological Bulletin, 101,* 213–232.

Adams, P. L. (1973). Functions of the lower-class partial family. *American Journal of Psychiatry, 130,* 200–203.

Adams, P. L., Milner, J. R., & Schrepf, N. A. (1984). *Fatherless children.* New York: Wiley & Sons.

Addington, J. (1992). Separation group. *Journal for Specialists in Group Work, 17,* 20–28.

Ahlburg, D. A., & DeVita, C. J. (1992). New realities of the American family. *Population Bulletin, 47*(2).

Ahrons, C. R. (1981). Continuing coparental relationship between divorced spouses. *American Journal of Orthopsychiatry, 5,* 415–428.

Ahrons, C. R., & Bowman, M. E. (1982). Changes in family relationships following divorce of adult child: Grandmother's perceptions. *Journal of Divorce, 5,* 49–68.

Ahrons, C. R., & Perlmutter, M. S. (1982). Therapy with remarriage families: III. The relationship between former spouses: A fundamental subsystem in the remarriage family. *Family Therapy Collections, 2,* 31–46.

Allison, P. D., & Furstenberg, F. F. (1989). How marital dissolution affects children: Variations by age and sex. *Developmental Psychology, 25,* 540–549.

Alpert-Gillis, L. J., Pedro-Carroll, J. L., & Cowen, E. L. (1989). The Children of Divorce Intervention Program: Development, implementation and evaluation of a program for young urban children. *Journal of Consulting and Clinical Psychology, 57,* 583–589.

Amato, P. R. (1987). Family processes in one-parent, stepparent, and intact families: The child's point of view. *Journal of Marriage and the Family, 49,* 327–337.

Amato, P. R. (1991). The "child of divorce" as a person prototype: Bias in the recall of information about children in divorced families. *Journal of Marriage and the Family, 53,* 59–69.

Amato, P. R., & Keith, B. (1991a). Parental divorce and the well-being of children: A meta-analysis. *Psychological Bulletin, 110,* 26–46.

Amato, P. R., & Keith, B. (1991b). Parental divorce and adult well-being: A meta-analysis. *Journal of Marriage and the Family, 53,* 43–58.

Ambert, A. M. (1986). Being a stepparent: Live-in and visiting stepchildren. *Journal of Marriage and the Family, 48,* 795–804.

American Psychiatric Association (1987). *Diagnostic and statistical manual of mental disorders: DSM III-R.* Washington, DC

Andrews, J. M. (1976). Delinquency, sex, and family variables. *Social Biology, 23*(2), 168–171.

Andrews, R. O., & Christensen, H. T. (1951). Relationship of absence of parent to courtship status: A repeat study. *American Sociological Review, 16,* 541–544.

Arditti, J. A. (1992). Differences between fathers with joint custody and noncustodial fathers. *American Journal of Orthopsychiatry, 62,* 186–195.

Austin, R. L. (1978). Race, father-absence, and female delinquency. *Criminology, 15*(4), 487–504.

Ball, D. W., Newman, J. M., & Scheuren, W. J. (1984). Teacher's generalized expectations of children of divorce. *Psychological Reports, 54,* 347–353.

Bandura, A. (1989). Human agency in social cognitive theory. *American Psychologist, 44,* 1175–1184.

Bandura, A., & Walters, R. (1963). *Social learning and personality development.* New York: Holt, Rinehart & Winston.

Bannon, J. A., & Southern, M. L. (1980). Father-absent women: Self-concept and modes of relating to men. *Sex Roles, 6,* 75–84.

Barber, B. L., & Eccles, J. S. (1992). Long-term influence of divorce and single parenting on adolescent family- and work-related values, behaviors, and aspirations. *Psychological Bulletin, 111,* 108–126.

Beardsall, L., & Dunn, J. (1992). Adversities in childhood: Siblings' experiences, and their relations to self-esteem. *Journal of Child Psychology and Psychiatry, 33,* 349–359.

Beer, J. (1989). Relationship of divorce to self-concept, self-esteem, and grade point average of fifth and sixth grade school children. *Psychological Reports, 65,* 1379–1383.

Belcastro, P. A., & Nicholson, T. (1989, November). *Latent effects of divorce in children's sexual experiences.* Presented at meeting of the Society for the Scientific Study of Sex.

Bell, N. J., Avery, A. W., Jenkins, D., Feld, U., & Schoenrock, C. J. (1985). Family relationships and social competence during late adolescence. *Journal of Youth and Adolescence, 14,* 109–119.

Belsky, J., Steinberg, L., & Draper, P. (1991). Childhood experience, interpersonal development, and reproductive strategy: An evolutionary theory of socialization. *Child Development, 62,* 647–670.

Bem, S. L. (1979). Theory and measurement of androgyny: A reply to the Pedhazur-Tetenbaum and Locksley-Colten critiques. *Journal of Personality and Social Psychology, 37,* 1047–1054.

Bem, S. L. (1981). Gender schema theory: A cognitive account of sex typing. *Psychological Review, 88,* 354–364.

Berger, A. S., & Simon, W. (1974). Black families and the Moynihan report: A research evaluation. *Social Problems, 22,* 145–161.

Berlinsky, E. B., & Biller, H. B. (1982). *Parental death and psychological development.* Lexington, MA: D. C. Heath.

Beverina, M. (1989). Parents' divorce, an ordeal for the child, cause or factor of possible psychopathological breakdown. *Annales Meicco Psychologiques, 147,* 210–214.

Biller, H. B. (1974). *Paternal deprivation: Family, school, sexuality, society.* Lexington, MA: D. C. Heath.

Biller, H. B. (1993). *Fathers and families: Paternal factors in child development.* Westport, CN: Auburn House.

Biller, H. B., & Solomon, R. S. (1986). *Child maltreatment and paternal deprivation.* Lexington, MA: D. C. Heath.

Billingsham, R. E., Pillion, L. A., & Sauer, A. K. (1991, November). *Family disruption and sexual attitudes and behaviors of college students.* Presented at meeting of the Society for the Scientific Study of Sex, New Orleans.

Bisnaire, L. M. C., Firestone, P., & Rynard, D. (1990). Factors associated with academic achievement in children following parental separation. *American Journal of Orthopsychiatry, 60*(1), 67–76.

Black, K. N. (1982). Consequences for offspring of single parent families. *Academic Psychology Bulletin, 4,* 527–534.

Black, K. N. (1985, March). *Parent-child relationships in families of divorce.* Paper presented at conference The Future of Parenting, Chicago.

Black, L. E., & Sprenkle, D. H. (1991). Gender differences in college students' attitudes toward divorce and their willingness to marry. *Journal of Divorce and Remarriage, 14,* 47–60.

Blechman, E. A. (1982). Are children with one parent at psychological risk? A methodological review. *Journal of Marriage and the Family, 44,* 179–195.

Block, J. H., Block, J., & Gjerde, P. F. (1986). The personality of children prior to divorce: A prospective study. *Child Development, 57,* 827–840.

Bloom, B. L., Asher, S. J., & White, S. W. (1978). Marital disruption as a stressor: A review and analysis. *Psychological Bulletin, 85,* 867–894.

Bloom, B. L., Hodges, W. F., & Caldwell, R. A. (1982). A preventive intervention program for the newly separated: Initial evaluation. *American Journal of Community Psychology, 10,* 251–264.

Bloom B. L., Hodges, W. F., Kern, M. B., & McFaddin, S. C. (1985). A preventive intervention program for the newly separated: Final evaluation. *American Journal of Orthopsychiatry, 55,* 9–26.

Bonkowski, S. E., Bequette, S. Q., & Boomhower, S. (1984). A group design to help children adjust to parental divorce. *Social Casework, 65,* 131–137.

Bonkowski, S. E., Boomhower, S., & Bequette, S. Q. (1985). What you don't know can hurt you: Unexpressed fears and feelings of children from divorcing families. *Journal of Divorce, 9,* 33–45.

Booth, A., Brinkerhoff, D. B., & White, L. K. (1984). The impact of parental divorce on courtship. *Journal of Marriage and the Family, 46*(1), 85–94.

Booth, A., & Edwards, J. N. (1989). Transmission of marital and family quality over the generations: The effect of parental divorce and unhappiness. *Journal of Divorce, 13,* 41–58.

Boss, P. (1986). Psychological absence in the intact family: A systems approach to a study of fathering. *Marriage & Family Review, 10*(1), 11–39.

Bowerman, C. E., & Irish, D. P. (1962). Some relationships of stepchildren to their parents. *Marriage and Family Living, 24,* 113–121.

Boyd, D. A., & Parish, T. (1984). An investigation of father loss and college students' androgyny scores. *Journal of Genetic Psychology, 145*(2), 279–280.

Boyd, D. A., & Parish, T. S. (1985). An examination of academic achievement in light of familial configuration. *Education, 106*(2), 228–230.

Brady, C. A., & Ambler, J. (1982). Use of group educational techniques with remarried couples. In L. Messinger (Ed.), *Therapy with remarried families* (pp. 145–157). Rockville, MD: Aspen System Corp.

Brandwein, R. A., Brown, C. A., & Fox, E. M. (1974). The social situation of divorced mothers and their families. *Journal of Marriage and the Family, 36*, 498–514.

Braver, S., Gonzalez, N., Sandler, I., & Wolchik, S. (1985, February). Economic hardship and postdivorce adjustment of custodial mothers. Paper presented to the Third Annual Conference on Family Competence, Arizona State University. Cited in Emery, R. E. (1988). *Marriage, divorce, and children's adjustment*. Newbury Park, CA: Sage.

Brenes, M. E., Eisenberg, N., & Helmstadter, G. C. (1985). Sex role development of preschoolers from two-parent and one-parent families. *Merrill-Palmer Quarterly, 31*, 33–46.

Brook, J. S., Whiteman, M., & Gordon, A. S. (1985). Father absence, perceived family characteristics and stage of drug use in adolescence. *British Journal of Developmental Psychology, 2*, 87–94.

Brook, J. S., Whiteman, M., Gordon, A. S., & Brook, D. W. (1984) Paternal determinants of female adolescent's marijuana use. *Developmental Psychology, 20*, 1032–1043.

Brooks-Gunn, J., & Furstenberg, F. F., Jr. (1986). The children of adolescent mothers: Physical, academic, and psychological outcomes. *Developmental Review, 6*, 224–251.

Brownfield, D. (1987). Father-son relationships and violent behavior. *Deviant Behavior, 8*, 65–78.

Browning, C. (1960). Differential impact of family disorganization on male adolescents. *Social Problems, 8*(1), 37–44.

Buchanan, C. M., Maccoby, E. E., & Dornbusch, S. M. (1991). Caught between parents: Adolescents' experience in divorced homes. *Child Development, 62*, 1008–1029.

Bullough, V. L. (1990). History and the understanding of human sexuality. In J. Bancroft (Ed.), *Annual Review of Sex Research, 1*, 75–92.

Bumpass, L. L., & Sweet, J. A. (1972). Differentials in marital instability: 1970. *American Sociological Review, 37*, 754–766.

Burns, A. (1992). Mother-headed families: An international perspective and the case of Australia. *Social Policy Report, 6*(1), 1–22.

Burstein, L. J. (1983). Daughters of divorce: Heterosexual-intimacy development in college females in relation to mothers' heterosexual attitudes. *Dissertation Abstracts International, 357B*. (University Microfilms No. 8311588).

Cafferata, G. L., & Kasper, J. D. (1985). Family structure and children's use of ambulatory physician services. *Medical Care, 23*, 350–360.

Camara, K. A., & Resnick, G. (1988). Interparental conflict and cooperation: Factors moderating children's post-divorce adjustment. In E. M. Hetherington & J. E. Arasteh (Eds.), *Impact of divorce, single parenting, and stepparenting on children* (pp. 166–195). Hillsdale, NJ: Erlbaum.

Campbell, D. T., & Stanley, J. C. (1963). *Experimental and quasi-experimental designs for research*. Boston: Houghton Mifflin.

Canter, R. J. (1982). Family correlates of male and female delinquency. *Criminology, 20*(2), 149–167.

Cantrell, R. G. (1986). Adjustment to divorce: Three components to assist children. *Elementary School Guidance and Counseling, 20,* 163–173.

Carlson, E. (1979). Family background, school and early marriage. *Journal of Marriage and the Family, 41,* 341–353.

Catton, W. R. (1988). Family "divorce heritage" and its intergenerational transmission: Toward a system-level perspective. *Sociological Perspectives, 31,* 398–419.

Cherian, V. I. (1989). Academic achievement of children of divorced parents. *Psychological Reports, 64,* 355–358.

Cherlin, A. J., Furstenberg, F. F., Jr., Chase-Lansdale, P. L., Kiernan, K. E., Robins, P. K., Morrison, D. R., & Teitler, J. O. (1991). Longitudinal studies of effects of divorce on children in Great Britain and the United States. *Science, 252,* 1386–1389.

Chilton, R. J., & Markle, G. E. (1972). Family disruption, delinquent conduct and the effect of subclassification. *American Sociological Review, 37,* 93–99.

Christensen, A., Johnson, S. M., Phillips, S., & Glasgow, R. E. (1980). Cost effectiveness in behavioral family therapy. *Behavior Therapy, 11,* 208–226.

Ciborowski, P. J. (1984). *The changing family: Group manual.* Port Charter, NY: Stratmar Educational Systems.

Cissna, K. N., Cox, D. E., & Bochner, A. P. (1990). The dialectic of marital and parental relationships within the stepfamily. *Communication Monographs, 57,* 44–61.

Clingempeel, W. G. (1981). Quasi-kin relationships and marital quality. *Journal of Personality and Social Psychology, 41,* 890–901.

Clingempeel, W. G., Brand, E., & Ievoli, R. (1984). Stepparent-stepchild relationships in stepmother and stepfather families: A multimethod study. *Family Relations Journal of Applied Family and Child Studies, 33,* 465–473.

Clingempeel, W. G., Colyar, J. J., Brand, E., & Hetherington, E. M. (1992). Children's relationships with maternal grandparents: A longitudinal study of family structure and pubertal status effects. *Child Development, 63,* 1404–1422.

Clingempeel, W. G., Ievoli, R., & Brand, E. (1984). Structural complexity and the quality of stepfather-stepchild relationships. *Family Process, 23,* 547–560.

Cockburn, J., & Maclay, I. (1965). Sex differentials in juvenile delinquency. *British Journal of Criminology, 5*(3), 289–308.

Cohen, J. (1977). *Statistical power analysis for the behavioral sciences* (rev. ed.). New York, Academic Press.

Cohen, J. (1983). The impact of marital dissolution on personal distress and child rearing attitudes of mothers. *Journal of Orthomolecular Psychiatry, 12,* 48–59.

Coleman, M., & Ganong, L. H. (1989). Financial management in stepfamilies. *Lifestyles, 10,* 217–232.

Colletta, N. D. (1983). Stressful lives: The situation of divorced mothers and their children. *Journal of Divorce, 6*(3), 19–31.

Collier, J. L. (1991). *The rise of selfishness in America.* New York: Oxford University Press.

Cook, A. S., & McBride, J. (1982). Divorce: Helping children cope. *School Counselor, 30,* 89–94.

Cooney, T. M. (1985). *Parental divorce in young adulthood: Implications for the parent-child relationship.* Unpublished master's thesis, Pennsylvania State University.

Cooney, T. M., Smyer, M. A., Hagestad, G. O., & Klock, R. (1986). Parental divorce in young adulthood: Some preliminary findings. *American Journal of Orthopsychiatry, 56,* 470–477.

Cooney, T. M., & Uhlenberg, P. (1990). The role of divorce in men's relations with their adult children after mid-life. *Journal of Marriage and the Family, 52*, 677–688.

Cowen, E. L., Hightower, A. D., Pedro-Carroll, J., & Work, W. C. (1989). School-based models for primary prevention programming with children. *Prevention in Human Services, 7*, 133–160.

Crook, T., & Eliot, J. (1980). Parental death during childhood and adult depression: A critical review of the literature. *Psychological Bulletin, 87*, 252–259.

Crosbie-Burnett, M. (1991). Impact of joint versus sole custody and quality of co-parental relationships on adjustment of adolescents in remarried families. *Behavioral Sciences and the Law, 9*, 439–449.

Cummings, E. M., Vogel, D., Cummings, J. S., & El-sheikh, M. (1989). Children's responses to different forms of expression of anger between adults. *Child Development, 60*, 1392–1404.

Datesman, S. K., & Scarpitti, F. R. (1975). Female delinquency and broken homes: A reassessment. *Criminology, 13*(1), 33–56.

Daum, J. M., & Bieliauskas, V. J. (1983). Fathers' absence and moral development of male delinquents. *Psychological Reports, 53*, 223–228.

Dentler, R. A., & Monroe, L. J. (1961). Social correlates of early adolescent theft. *American Sociological Review, 26*, 733–743.

Desimone-Luis, J., O'Mahoney, K., & Hunt, D. (1979). Children of separation and divorce: Factors influencing adjustment. *Journal of Divorce, 3*, 37–42.

Doherty, W. J., & Needle, R. H. (1991). Psychological adjustment and substance use among adolescents before and after a parental divorce. *Child Development, 62*, 328–337.

Dolan, B. M., Lieberman, S., Evans, C., & Lacey, J. H. (1990). Family features associated with normal body weight bulimia. *International Journal of Eating Disorders, 9*, 639–647.

Donnelly, D., & Finklehor, D. (1992). Does equality in custody arrangement improve the parent-child relationship? *Journal of Marriage and the Family, 54*, 837–845.

Dornbusch, S. M., Carlsmith, J. M., Bushwall, S. J., Ritter, P. L., Leiderman, H., Hastorf, A. H., & Gross, R. T. (1985). Single parents, extended households, and the control of adolescents. *Child Development, 56*, 326–341.

Downey, D. B., & Powell, B. (1993). Do children in single-parent households fare better living with same-sex parents? *Journal of Marriage and the Family, 55*, 55–71.

Dubow, E. F., & Tisak, J. (1989). The relation between stressful life events and adjustment in elementary school children: The role of social support and social problems-solving skills. *Child Development, 60*, 1412–1423.

Duncan, G. J., & Hoffman, S. D. (1985). Economic consequences of marital instability. In M. David & T. Smeeding (Eds.), *Horizontal equity, uncertainy and wellbeing* (pp. 427–469). Chicago: University of Chicago Press.

Dusek, J. B. (1987). Sex roles and adjustment. In D. B. Carter (Eds.), *Current Conceptions of Sex Roles and Sex Typing* (pp. 211–222). New York: Praeger.

Earl, L., & Lohmann, N. (1978). Absent fathers and black male children. *Social Work, 23*, 413–415.

Earl, W. L. (1987). Creativity and self-trusts: A field study. *Adolescence, 22*, 419–432.

Eberhardt, C. A., & Schill, T. (1984). Differences in sexual attitudes and likeliness of sexual behaviors of black lower-socioeconomic father-present vs. father-absent female adolescents. *Adolescence, 19*, 99–105.

Eisendorfer, A. (1943). The clinical significance of the single parent relationships in women. *Psychoanalytic Quarterly, 12*, 223–239.

Elkind, D. (1986). Stress and the middle grader. *School Counselor, 33*, 196–206.

Emery, R. E. (1982). Interparental conflict and the children of discord and divorce. *Psychological Bulletin, 92*(2), 310–330.

Emery, R. E., Hetherington, E. M., & DiLalla, C. F. (1984). Divorce, children, and social policy. In A. E. Siegel & H. W. Stevenson (Eds.), *Child development and social policy* (pp. 189–266). Chicago: University of Chicago Press.

Emery, R. E., & Wyer, M. M. (1987). Divorce mediation. *American Psychologist, 42*, 472–480.

Eno, M. M. (1985). Sibling relationships in families of divorce. *Journal of Psychotherapy and the Family, 1*, 139–156.

Epstein, Y. M., Borduin, C. M., & Wexler, A. S. (1985). The Children Helping Children Program: A case illustration. *Special Services in the School, 2*, 73–93.

Farnworth, M. (1984). Family structure, family attributes, and delinquency in a sample of low-income, minority males and females. *Journal of Youth and Adolescence, 13*(4) 349–365.

Fassel, D. (1991). *Growing up divorced*. New York: Pocket Books.

Fauber, R., Forehand, R., Thomas, A. M., & Wierson, M. (1990). A mediational model of the impact of marital conflict on adolescent adjustment in intact and divorced families: The role of disrupted parenting. *Child Development, 61*, 1112–1123.

Fendrich, M., Warner, V., & Weissman, M. M. (1990). Family risk factors, parental depression, and psychopathology in offspring. *Developmental Psychology, 26*, 40–50.

Ferguson, D. M., Horwood, L. J., & Lynskey, M. T. (1992). Family change, parental discord, and early offending. *Journal of Child Psychology and Psychiatry, 33*, 1059–1075.

Ferri, E. (1976). *Growing up in a one-parent family: A long-term study of child development*. London: National Foundation for Education Research.

Fichter, M. M., & Noegel, R. (1990). Concordance rates for bulimia nervosa in twins. *International Journal of Eating Disorders, 9*, 255–263.

Fidler, B. J., & Saunders, E. B. (1988). Children's adjustment during custody-access disputes: Relation to custody arrangement, gender, and age of child. *Canadian Journal of Psychiatry, 33*, 517–523.

Fine, M. A., Moreland, J. R., & Schwebel, A. I. (1983). Long-term effects of divorce on parent-child relationships. *Developmental Psychology, 19*, 703–713.

Fine, M. A., & Schwebel, A. I. (1987). An emergent explanation of differing racial reactions to single parenthood. *Journal of Divorce, 11*, 1–15.

Finkelhor, D., Hotaling, G. T., & Selak, A. J. (1992). The abduction of children by strangers and nonfamily members: Estimating the incidence using multiple methods. *Journal of Interpersonal Violence, 7*, 226–243.

Fintushel, N., & Hillard, N. (1991). *A grief out of season*. Boston: Little, Brown.

Fisher, H. (1990, November) *The evolution of monogamy, adultery, and divorce*. Paper presented for the Society for the Scientific Study of Sex.

Fleck, J. R., Fuller, C. C., Malin, S. Z., Miller, D. H., & Acheson, K. R. (1980). Father psychological absence and heterosexual behavior, personal adjustment and sex-typing in adolescent girls. *Adolescence, 15*, 847–860.

Forehand, R., Brody, G., Long, N., Slotkin, J., & Fauber, R. (1986). Divorce/divorce potential and interparental conflict: The relationship to early adolescent social and cognitive functioning. *Journal of Adolescent Research, 4*, 389–397.

Forehand, R., Wierson, M., Thomas, A. M., Armistead, L., Kempton, T., & Fauber, R. (1990). Interparental conflict and paternal visitation following divorce: The interactive effect on adolescent competence. *Child Study Journal, 20*(3), 193–202.

Forgatch, M. S., Patterson, G. R., & Skinner (1988). A mediational model for the effect of divorce on antisocial behavior in boys. In E. M. Hetherington & J. D. Arasteh (Eds.), *Impact of divorce, single parenting and step-parenting on children* (pp. 135–154). Hillsdale, NJ: Erlbaum.

Fox, N. A., Kimmerly, N. L., & Schafer, W. D. (1991). Attachment to mother/attachment to father: A meta-analysis. *Child Development, 62,* 1–22.

Franklin, K. M., Janoff-Bulman, R., & Roberts, J. E. (1990). Long-term impact of parental divorce on optimism and trust: Changes in general assumptions or narrow beliefs? *Journal of Personality and Social Psychology, 59,* 743–755.

Freud, S. (1949). The passing of the Oedipus complex. In E. Jones (Ed.), *Collected papers* (Vol. 2). London: Hogarth Press. (Original work published 1924)

Freud, S. (1950). Some consequences of the anatomical distinction between the sexes. In E. Jones (Ed.), *Collected papers.* (Vol. 5). London: Hogarth Press. (Original work published 1925)

Fry, P. S. (1983). Father absence and deficits in children's social-cognitive development: Implications for intervention and training. *Journal of Psychiatric Treatment and Evaluation, 5,* 113–120.

Fry, P. S., & Scher, A. (1984). The effects of father absence on children's achievement motivation, ego-strength, and locus-of-control orientation: A five-year longitudinal assessment. *British Journal of Developmental Psychology, 2,* 167–178.

Furstenberg, F. F. (1988). Child care after divorce and remarriage. In E. M. Hetherington & J. D. Arasteh (Eds.), *Impact of divorce, single parenting, and stepparenting on children* (pp. 245–261). Hillsdale, NJ: Erlbaum.

Furstenberg, F. F., & Cherlin, A. J. (1991). *Divided Families: What happens to children when parents part.* Cambridge: Harvard University Press.

Furstenberg, F. F., Morgan, S. P., & Allison, P. D. (1987). Paternal participation and children's well-being after marital dissolution. *American Sociological Review, 52,* 695–701.

Furstenberg, F. F., Peterson, J. L., Nord, C. W., & Zill, N. (1983). The life course of children of divorce: Marital disruption and parental contact. *American Sociological Review, 48,* 656–668.

Furstenberg, F. F., & Spanier, G. B. (1984). *Recycling the family: Remarriage after divorce.* Beverly Hills: Sage.

Furstenberg, F. F., & Zill, N. (1984). A national longitudinal study of marital disruption. Synopsis. Washington, DC: Child Trends Inc. Cited in E. M. Hetherington & J. D. Arasteh (Eds.), *Impact of divorce, single parenting, and stepparenting on children.* Hillsdale, NJ: Erlbaum.

Ganong, L. H., & Coleman, M. M. (1987). Stepchildren's perceptions of their parents. *Journal of Genetic Psychology, 148,* 5–17.

Ganong, L. H., Coleman, M., & Brown, G. (1981). Effect of family structure on marital attitudes of adolescents. *Adolescence, 16,* 281–288.

Gardner, R. A. (1970). *Boys and girls book about divorce.* New York: Bantam Books.

Gardner, R. (1989). *Family evaluation in child custody mediation, arbitration and litigation.* Cresskill, NJ: Creative Therapeutics.

Garvin, V., Leber, D., & Kalter, N. (1991). Children of divorce: Predictors of change following preventive intervention. *American Journal of Orthopsychiatry, 61,* 438–447.

Gay, M. J., & Tonge, W. L. (1967). The late effects of loss of parents in childhood. *British Journal of Psychiatry, 113*, 753–759.

Gelles, R. J. (1989). Child abuse and violence in single-parent families: Parental absence and economic deprivation. *American Journal of Orthopsychiatry, 59*, 492–501.

Gendler, M. (1986). Group puppetry with school-age children: Rational, procedure and therapeutic implication. *Arts in Psychotherapy, 13*, 45–52.

Gibson, H. B. (1969). Early delinquency in relation to broken homes. *Journal of Child Psychology and Psychiatry, 10*, 195–204.

Gispert, M., Brinich, P., Wheeler, K., Krieger, L. (1984). Predictors of repeat pregnancies among low-income adolescents. *Hospital and Community Psychiatry, 35*, 719–723.

Glass, B. V., McGaw, B., & Smith, M. L. (1981). *Meta-analysis in social research.* Beverly Hills, CA: Sage.

Glenn, N. D., & Kramer, K. B. (1985). The psychological well-being of adult children of divorce. *Journal of Marriage and the Family, 47*, 905–912.

Glenn, N. D., & Kramer, K. B. (1987). The marriages and divorces of the children of divorce. *Journal of Marriage and the Family, 49*, 811–825.

Glenn, N. D., & Shelton, B. A. (1983). Pre-adult background variables and divorce: A note of caution about overreliance on explained variance. *Journal of Marriage and the Family, 45*, 405–410.

Glover, R. J., & Steele, C. (1989). Comparing the effects on the child of post-divorce parenting arrangements. In C. A. Everett, (Ed.), *Children of divorce: Developmental and clinical issues* (pp. 185–201). New York: Haworth.

Goldenberg, I., & Goldenberg, H. (1985). *Family Therapy: An Overview* (2nd ed.). Monterey, CA: Brooks/Cole.

Goldstein, J., Freud, A., & Solnit, A. (1973). *Beyond the best interests of the child.* New York: MacMillan.

Goldstein-Henaday, S., Green, V., & Evans, J. R. (1986). Effects of teachers' marital status and child's family's marital status on teachers ratings of a child. *Psychological Reports, 58*, 959–964.

Golombok, S., Spencer, A., & Rutter, M. (1983). Children in lesbian and single-parent households: Psychosexual and psychiatric appraisal. *Journal of Child Psychology and Psychiatry, 24*(4), 551–572.

Greenberg, E. F., & Nay, W. R. (1982). The intergenerational transmission of marital instability reconsidered. *Journal of Marriage and the Family, 44*, 335–347.

Greenfeld, N., & Teevan, R. C. (1986). Fear of failure in families without fathers. *Psychological Reports, 59*, 571–574.

Gregory, I. A. (1965). Anterospective data following childhood loss of a parent: II. Pathology, performance and potential among college studies. *Archives of General Psychiatry, 13*, 110–120.

Greif, G. L. (1990). *The daddy track and the single father.* Lexington, MA: Lexington Books.

Greif, G. L., & Hegar, R. L. (1993). *When parents kidnap: The families behind the headlines.* New York: Free Press.

Greif, G. L., & Pabst, M. S. (1988). *Mothers without custody.* Lexington, MA: Lexington Books.

Griggs, S. A. (1968). A study of the life plans of culturally disadvantaged negro adolescent girls with father-absence in the home. *Dissertation Abstracts International, 28*, 4950A. (University Microfilms No. 68–8979)

Grych, J. H., & Fincham, F. D. (1992). Interventions for children of divorce: Toward greater integration of research and action. *Psychological Bulletin, 111*, 434–454.

Guidubaldi, J., & Cleminshaw, H. K. (1985). Divorce, family health, and child adjustment. *Family Relations Journal of Applied Family and Child Studies, 34,* 36–41.

Guidubaldi, J., Cleminshaw, H., & Perry, J. (1985). The relationship of parental divorce to health status of parents and children. *Special Services in the Schools, 1*(3), 73–87.

Guidubaldi, J., & Perry, J. D. (1985). Divorce and mental health sequelae for children: A two-year follow-up of a nationwide sample. *Journal of the American Academy of Child Psychiatry, 24,* 531–537.

Gurman, A. S., Kniskern, D. P., & Pinsof, W. M. (1986). Research on marital and family therapies. In S. L. Garfield & A. E. Bergin (Eds.), *Handbook of psychotherapy and behavior change* (pp. 565–626). New York: Wiley.

Guttman, J. (1987). Test anxiety and performance of adolescent children of divorced parents. *Educational Psychology, 7,* 225–229.

Guttman, J. (1989). Intimacy in young adult males' relationships as a function of divorced and non-divorced family of origin structure. *Journal of Divorce, 12*(2–3), 253–261.

Guttman, J., Amir, T., & Katz, M. (1987). Threshold of withdrawal from schoolwork among children of divorced parents. *Educational Psychology, 7*(4), 295–302.

Guttman, J., & Broudo, M. (1989). The effect of children's family type on teachers' stereotypes. In C. A. Everett (Ed.), *Children of divorce: Developmental and clinical issues* (pp. 315–328). New York: Haworth.

Guttman, J., Geva, N., & Gefen, S. (1988). Teachers' and school children's stereotypic perception of "the child of divorce." *American Educational Research Journal, 25,* 555–571.

Gwynn, C. A., & Brantley, H. T. (1987). Effect of a divorce group intervention for elementary school children. *Psychology in the Schools, 24,* 161–164.

Haffey, M., & Cohen, P. M. (1992). Treatment issues for divorcing women. *Families in Society, 73,* 142–148.

Hainline, L., & Feig, E. (1978). The correlates of childhood father absence in college-aged women. *Child Development, 49,* 37–42.

Hammond, J. (1981). *Group counseling for children of divorce: A guide for the elementary school.* Ann Arbor, MI: Cranbrook.

Hampton, R. (1975). Labeling theory and the police decision to prosecute juveniles. *Australian and New Zealand Journal of Sociology, 11*(3), 64–66.

Harvey, V. S. (1991). Characteristics of children referred to school psychologists: A discriminant analysis. *Psychology in the Schools, 28,* 209–218.

Haurin, R. J. (1992). Patterns of childhood residence and the relationship to young adult outcomes. *Journal of Marriage and the Family, 54,* 846–860.

Hawkins, A. J., & Eggebeen, D. J. (1991). Are fathers fungible? Patterns of coresident adult men in maritally disrupted families and young children's well-being. *Journal of Marriage and Family, 53,* 958–972.

Hayes, R. (1989). Men in female-concentrated occupations. *Journal of Organizational Behavior, 10,* 201–212.

Heady, B., & Wearing, A. (1989). Personality, life events, and subjective well-being: Toward a dynamic equilibrium model. *Journal of Personality and Social Psychology, 57,* 731–739.

Heckel, R. V. (1963). The effects of fatherlessness on the preadolescent female. *Mental Hygiene, 47*, 69–73.

Hegar, R. L., & Greif, G. L. (1991). Abduction of children by their parents: A survey of the problem. *Social Work, 36*, 421–426.

Heiss, J. (1972). On the transmission of marital instability in black families. *American Sociological Review, 37*, 82–92.

Hennessy, M., Richards, P. J., & Berk, R. (1978). Broken homes and middle-class delinquency: A reassessment. *Criminology, 15*(4), 505–527.

Hepworth, J., Ryder, R. G., & Dreyer, A. S. (1984). The effects of parental loss on the formation of intimate relationships. *Journal of Marital and Family Therapy, 10*, 73–82.

Herzog, E., & Sudia, C. E. (1973). Children in fatherless families. In B. Caldwell & H. Ricciuti (Eds.), *Review of child development research* (Vol. 3) (pp. 141–232). Chicago: University of Chicago Press.

Hess, R. D., & Camara, K. A. (1979). Post-divorce family relations as mediating factors in the consequences of divorce for children. *Journal of Social Issues, 35*, 79–96.

Hetherington, E. M. (1972). Effects of father absence on personality development in adolescent daughters. *Developmental Psychology, 7*, 313–326.

Hetherington, E. M. (1973, Feb). Girls without fathers. *Psychology Today*, 47–52.

Hetherington, E. M. (1988). Parents, children, and siblings six years after divorce. In R. Hinde & J. Stevenson-Hinde (Eds.), *Relationships within families*. Cambridge: Cambridge University Press.

Hetherington, E. M. (1989). Coping with family transitions: Winners, losers, and survivors. *Child Development, 60*, 1–14.

Hetherington, E. M., Camara, K. A., & Featherman, D. L. (1983). Achievement and intellectual functioning of children in one-parent households. In J. T. Spence (Ed.), *Achievement and achievement motives* (pp. 205–284). San Francisco: W. H. Freeman.

Hetherington, E. M., Cox, M., & Cox, R. (1978). The aftermath of divorce. In J. H. Stevens & M. Matthews (Eds.), *Mother-child, father-child relations* (pp. 110–155). Washington, DC: National Association for the Education of Young Children.

Hetherington, E. M., Cox, M., & Cox, R. (1981). *Cognitive performance, school behavior, and achievement of children from one-parent households*. Washington, DC: National Institute of Education. (ERIC Document Reproduction Service No. ED 321 721).

Hetherington, E. M., Cox, M., & Cox, R. (1982). Effects of divorce on parents and children. In M. E. Lamb (Ed.), *Nontraditional families*. Hillsdale, NJ: Erlbaum.

Hetherington, E. M., & Deur, J. I. (1971). The effects of father absence on child development. *Young Children, 26*, 233–248.

Hetherington, E. M., & Parke, R. (1979). *Child Psychology: A contemporary viewpoint* (2nd ed.). New York: McGraw-Hill.

Hodges, W. F., Wechsler, R. C., & Ballantine, C. (1979). Divorce and the preschool child: Cumulative stress. *Journal of Divorce, 3*, 55–67.

Hofmann, R., & Zippco, D. (1986). Effects of divorce upon school self-esteem and achievement of 10-, 11-, and 12-year-old children. *Perceptual and Motor Skills, 62*, 397–398.

Hoffman, M. L. (1971). Father absence and conscience development. *Developmental Psychology, 4*(3), 400–406.

Hogan, D. P., & Kitagawa, E. M. (1985). The impact of social status, family structure, and neighborhood on the fertility of black adolescents. *American Journal of Sociology, 90,* 825–855.

Holden, N. L., & Robinson, P. H. (1988). Anorexia nervosa and bulimia nervosa in British blacks. *British Journal of Psychiatry, 152,* 544–549.

Huddleston, R. J., & Hawkings, L. (1986). The effects of divorce: A study of the reports of divorced Albertans. *Conciliation Courts Review, 24,* 59–68.

Huston, A. C. (1983). Sex-typing. In E. M. Hetherington (Ed.), P. H. Mussen (Series Ed.), *Handbook of child psychology* (4th ed., Vol. 4, pp. 387–467). New York: Wiley.

Hutchinson, R. L., & Spangler-Hirsch, S. L. (1989). Children of divorce and single-parent lifestyles: Facilitating well-being. In C. A. Everett (Ed.), *Children of divorce: Developmental and clinical issues* (pp. 5–24). New York: Haworth.

Igoin-Apfelbaum, L. (1985). Characteristics of family background in bulimics. *Psychotherapy and Psychosomatic, 43*(3), 161–167.

Igoin-Apfelbaum, L., & Apfelbaum, M. (1990). Incidence of broken home family background in bulimia. *British Review of Bulimia and Anorexia Nervosa, 4,* 55–59.

Illsley, R., & Thompson, B. (1961). Women from broken homes. *Sociological Review, 9,* 27–54.

Isaacs, M. B., Leon, G., & Donohue, A. M. (1986). Who are the "normal" children of divorce? On the need to specify population. *Journal of Divorce, 10,* 107–119.

Isaacs, M. B., Leon, G., & Kline, M. (1987). When is a parent out of the picture? Different custody, different perceptions. *Family Process, 26,* 101–110.

Isaacs, M. B., Montalvo, B., & Abelsohn, D. (1986). *The difficult divorce.* New York: Basic Books.

Jacobson, B., & Ryder, R. G. (1969). Parental loss and some characteristics of the early marriage relationship. *American Journal of Orthopsychiatry, 39,* 779–787.

Jacobson, D. (1978). The impact of marital separation/divorce on children: I. Parent-child separation and child adjustment. *Journal of Divorce, 1,* 341–360.

Jennings, A. J., & Sheldon, M. G. (1985). Review of the health of children in one-parent families. *Journal of the Royal College of General Practitioners, 35,* 478–483.

Johnston, J. R., & Campbell, L. E. G. (1988). *Impasses of divorce: The dynamics and resolution of family conflict.* New York: Free Press.

Johnston, J. R., Kline, M., & Tschann, J. M. (1989). Ongoing postdivorce conflict: Effects of children of joint custody and frequent access. *American Journal of Orthopsychiatry, 59,* 576–592.

Jones, G. P. (1990). The boy is father to the man: A men's studies exploration of intergenerational interaction. *Men's Studies Review, 7,* 9–13.

Jones, S. M. (1978). Divorce and remarriage: A new beginning, a new set of problems. *Journal of Divorce, 2,* 217–227.

Jones, W. H., Cohn, M. G., & Miller, C. E. (1991). Betrayal among children and adults. In K. J. Rotenberg (Ed.), *Children's interpersonal trust* (pp. 118–134). New York: Springer-Verlag.

Jouriles, E. N., Pfiffner, L. J., & O'Leary, S. G. (1988). Marital conflict, parenting, and toddler conduct problems. *Journal of Abnormal Child Psychology, 16,* 197–206.

Jupp, J. J., & Purcell, I. P. (1992). A school-based group programme to uncover and change the problematic beliefs of children from divorced families. *School Psychology International, 13,* 17–29.

Kagel, S. A., & Schilling, K. M. (1985). Sexual identification and gender identity among father-absent males. *Sex Roles, 13*(5/6), 357–370.

Kalter, N. (1984). Conjoint mother-daughter treatment: A beginning phase of psychotherapy with adolescent daughters of divorce. *Journal of Orthopsychiatry, 54,* 490–497.

Kalter, N. (1987). Long-term effects of divorce on children. *American Journal of Orthopsychiatry, 57,* 587–600.

Kalter, N. (1990). *Growing up with divorce.* New York: Free Press.

Kalter, N., Riemer, B., Brickman, A., & Chen, J. W. (1985). Implications of parental divorce for female development. *Journal of the American Academy of Child Psychiatry, 24,* 538–544.

Kaminsky, H. (1986). The divorce adjustment education and support group for children. *Conciliation Courts Reviews, 24,* 45–49.

Kanoy, K. W., & Cunningham, J. L. (1984). Consensus of confusion in research on children and divorce: Conceptual and methodological issues. *Journal of Divorce, 7,* 45–71.

Kantrowitz, B. (1992, January 13). Breaking the divorce cycle. *Newsweek,* pp. 48–53.

Kaye, S. H. (1988–1989). The impact of divorce on children's academic performance. *Journal of Divorce, 12*(2/3), 283–298.

Keiser, S. (1953). A manifest Oedipus complex in an adolescent girl. *Psychoanalytic Study of the Child, 8,* 99–107.

Keith, V. M., & Finlay, B. (1988). The impact of parental divorce on children's educational attainment, marital timing and likelihood of divorce. *Journal of Marriage and the Family, 50,* 797–809.

Kendler, K. S., Neale, M. C., Kessler, R. C., Heath, A. C., & Eaves, L. J. (1992). Childhood parental loss and adult psychopathology in women: A tin study perspective. *Archives of General Psychiatry, 49,* 109–116.

Kenny, J. A., & Black, K. N. (undated). *Helping children of divorce.* Cincinnati: St. Anthony Messenger.

Kestenbaum, C. J., & Stone, M. H. (1976). The effects of fatherless homes upon daughters: Clinical impressions regarding paternal deprivation. *Journal of the American Academy of Psychoanalysis, 4,* 171–190.

Kimmons, L., & Gaston, J. A. (1986). Single parenting: A filmography. *Family Relations Journal of Applied Family and Child Studies, 35,* 205–211.

Kinard, E. M., & Reinherz, H. (1986). Effects of marital disruption on children's school aptitude and achievement. *Journal of Marriage and the Family, 48*(2), 285–293.

Kinnard, K., & Gerrard, M. (1986). Premarital sexual behavior and attitudes toward marriage among young women as a function of their mother's marital status. *Journal of Marriage and the Family, 48,* 757–765.

Kirkpatrick, K. (1992). *The effects of parental divorce on offspring interpersonal trust.* Unpublished master's thesis, Purdue University.

Kitson, G. C., & Raschke, J. J. (1981). Divorce research: What we know; what we need to know. *Journal of Divorce, 4,* 1–37.

Klee, L., Schmidt, C., & Johnson, C. (1989). Children's definitions of family following divorce of their parents. In C. A. Everett, (Ed.), *Children of divorce: Developmental and clinical issues.* New York: Haworth.

Kline, M., Tschann, J. M., Johnston, J. R., & Wallerstein, J. S. (1989). Children's adjustment in joint and sole physical custody families. *Developmental Psychology, 25,* 430–438.

Kohlberg, L. (1966). A cognitive-developmental analysis of children's sex-role concepts and attitudes. In E. E. Maccoby (Ed.), *The development of sex differences* (pp. 82–173). Stanford: Stanford University Press.

Krein, S. F., & Beller, A. H. (1988). Educational attainment of children from single-parent families: Differences by exposure, gender and race. *Demography, 25,* 221–224.

Kruk, E. (1992). Psychological and structural factors contributing to the disengagement of noncustodial fathers after divorce. *Family and Conciliation Courts Review, 30,* 81–101.

Kulka, R. A., & Weingarten, H. (1979). The long-term effects of parental divorce in children on adult adjustment. *Journal of Social Issues, 35*(4), 50–78.

Kurdek, L. A. (1981). An integrative perspective on children's divorce adjustment. *American Psychologist, 38*(8), 856–866.

Kurdek, L. A., & Berg, B. (1983). Correlations of children's adjustment to their parents' divorces. In L. A. Kurdek (Ed.), *Children and divorce: New directions for child development.* San Francisco: Jossey-Bass.

Kurdek, L. A., Blisk, D., & Siesky, A. E. (1981). Correlations of children's long-term adjustment to their parents' divorce. *Developmental Psychology, 17,* 565–579.

Kurdek, L. A., & Siesky, A. E. (1980). Sex role self concepts of single divorced parents and their children. *Journal of Divorce, 3,* 249–261.

Lahey, B. B., Hartdagen, S. E., Frick, P. J., McBurnett, K., Connor, R., & Hynd, G. W. (1988). Conduct disorder: Parsing the confounded relation to parental divorce and antisocial personality. *Journal of Abnormal Psychology, 97*(3), 334–337.

Lamers, W. M., Jr. (1977). The effects of father absence on children. In E. V. Stein (Ed.), *Fathering: Fact or fable* (pp. 68–86). Nashville, TN: Abingdon.

Landis, J. T. (1962). A comparison of children from divorced and nondivorced unhappy marriages. *Family Life Coordinator, 11,* 61–65.

Lansky, V. (1991). *Vicki Lansky's divorce books for parents.* New York: Signet.

LeCroy, C. W. (1988). Parent-adolescent intimacy: Impact on adolescent functioning. *Adolescence, 23,* 137–147.

Leonard, M. R. (1966). Fathers and daughters: The significance of 'fathering' in the psychosexual development of the girl. *International Journal of Psycho-Analysis, 47,* 325–334.

Levin, M. L. (1989). Sequelae to marital disruption in children. *Journal of Divorce, 12*(2–3), 25–80.

Levine, E. (1981). Teachers' academic and psychosocial expectations for children from single-parent families. *Dissertation Abstracts International, 41,* 533A.

Light, R. J., & Pillemer, D. B. (1984). *Summing up: The science of reviewing research.* Cambridge, MA: Harvard University Press.

Livingston, R. B., & Kordinak, S. T. (1990). The long term effect of parental divorce: Marital role expectations. *Journal of Divorce and Remarriage, 14,* 91–105.

Lohr, R., Legg, C., Mendell, A. E., & Riemer, B. S. (1989). Clinical observations on interferences of early father absence in the achievement of femininity. *Clinical Social Work Journal, 17*(4), 351–365.

Long, B. H. (1983). Evaluations and intentions concerning marriage among unmarried female undergraduates. *Journal of Social Psychology, 119,* 235–242.

Long, N., & Forehand, R. (1987). The effects of parental divorce and parental conflict on children: An overview. *Journal of Developmental and Behavioral Pediatrics, 8,* 292–296.

Long, N., Forehand, R., Fauber, R., & Brody, G. H. (1987). Self-perceived and independently observed competence of young adolescents as a function of parental marital conflict and recent divorce. *Journal of Abnormal Child Psychology, 15*(1), 15–27.

Love-Clark, P. (1984). A meta-analysis of the effects of divorce on children's adjustment. *Dissertation Abstracts International, 45,* 2807A.

Lowenstein, J. S., & Koopman, E. J. (1978). A comparison of self-esteem between boys living with single-parent mother and single-parent father. *Journal of Divorce, 2,* 195–208.

Lowery, C. R. (1986). Maternal and joint custody: Differences in the decision process. *Law and Human Behavior, 10,* 303–315.

Luepnitz, D. A. (1978). Children of divorce: A review of psychological literature. *Law and Human Behavior, 2,* 167–179.

Luepnitz, D. A. (1979). Which aspects of divorce affect children? *Family Coordinator, 28,* 79–85.

Luepnitz, D. A. (1982). *Child custody: A study of families after divorce.* Lexington, MA: Lexington Books.

Lynn, D. B. (1974). The absent father. In *The father: His role in child development* (pp. 254–280). Belmont, CA: Wadsworth.

Maccoby, E. E., Depner, C. E., & Mnookin, R. H. (1988). Custody of children following divorce. In E. M. Hetherington & J. D. Arasteh (Eds.), *Impact of divorce, single parenting, and stepparenting on children* (pp. 91–114). Hillsdale, NJ: Erlbaum.

MacKinnon C. E. (1988–89). Sibling interactions in married and divorced families: Influence of ordinal position, socioeconomic status, and play context. *Journal of Divorce, 12,* 221–234.

MacKinnon, C. E., Brody, G. H., & Stoneman, Z. (1982). The effects of divorce and maternal employment on the home environments of preschool children. *Child Development, 53,* 1392–1399.

MacKinnon, C. E., Brody, G. H., & Stoneman, Z. (1986). The longitudinal effects of divorce and maternal employment on the home environments of preschool children. *Journal of Divorce, 9*(4), 65–78.

Magura, M., & Shapiro, E. (1988). Alcohol consumption and divorce: Which causes which? *Journal of Divorce, 12,* 127–136.

Martin, C. L., & Halverson, C. F., Jr. (1981). A schematic processing model of sex typing and stereotyping in children. *Child Development, 52,* 1119–1134.

Martin, T. C., & Bumpass, L. L. (1989). Recent trends in marital disruption. *Demography, 26,* 37–51.

Matsueda, R. L., & Heimer, K. (1987). Race, family structure, and delinquency: A test of differential association and social control theories. *American Sociological Review, 52,* 827–840.

McCombs, A., & Forehand, R. (1989). Adolescent school performance following parental divorce: Are there family factors that can enhance success? *Adolescence, 24,* 871–880.

McCord, J., McCord, W., & Thurber, E. (1962). Some effects of paternal absence on male children. *Journal of Abnormal and Social Psychology, 64,* 361–369.

McCord, W., & McCord, J. (1959). *Origins of Crime.* New York: Columbia University Press.

McCranie, E. W., & Kahan, J. (1986). Personality and multiple divorce: A prospective study. *Journal of Nervous and Mental Disease, 176,* 161–164.

McDermott, J. F. (1968). Parental divorce in early childhood. *American Journal of Psychiatry, 124*, 1424–1432.

McGue, M., & Lykken, D. T. (1992). Genetic influence on risk of divorce. *Psychological Science, 3*, 368–373.

McLanahan, S. S. (1985). Family structure and the reproduction of poverty. *American Journal of Sociology, 90*, 873–901.

McLanahan, S. S., & Booth, K. (1989). Mother-only families: Problems, prospects, and politics. *Journal of Marriage and the Family, 51*, 557–580.

McLanahan, S. S., & Bumpass, L. (1988). Intergenerational consequences of family disruption. *American Journal of Sociology, 94*, 130–152.

McLeod, M., & Vonk, B. (1992). A support group for single-parent graduate students and their children. *Journal of College Student Development, 33*, 184–185.

McLoughlin, D., & Whitfield, R. (1984). Adolescents and their experience of parental divorce. *Journal of Adolescence, 7*, 155–170.

Meehan, P. J., Saltzman, L. E., & Sattin, R. W. (1991). Suicides among older United States residents: Epidemiologic characteristics and trends. *American Journal of Public Health, 81*, 1198–1200.

Meiss, M. L. (1952). The oedipal problem of a fatherless child. *Psychoanalytic Study of the Child, 7*, 216–229.

Michael, R. T., & Tuma, N. B. (1985). Entry into marriage and parenthood by young men and women: The influence of family background. *Demography, 22*, 515–544.

Miller, D. R. (1986). Sensitizing new teachers about father-absent boys. *Action in Teacher Education, 8*(3), 73–78.

Mills, D. M. (1984). A model for stepfamily development. *Family Relations Journal of Applied Family and Child Studies, 33*, 365–372.

Mischel, W. (1966). A social-learning view of sex differences in behavior. In E. Maccoby (Ed.), *The development of sex differences* (pp. 56–81). Stanford: Stanford University Press.

Mischel, W. (1970). Sex tying and socialization. In P. Mussen (Ed.). *Carmichael's manual of child psychology* (Vol. 2) (pp. 3–72). New York: Wiley.

Monahan, T. P. (1957). Family status and the delinquent child: A reappraisal and some new findings. *Social Forces, 35*, 250–258.

Moran, P., & Barclay, A. (1988). Effect of fathers' absence on delinquent boys: Dependency and hypermasculinity. *Psychological Reports, 62*, 115–121.

Moreno, C. A. (1989). Utilization of medical services by single-parent and two-parent families. *Journal of Family Practice, 28*, 194–199.

Morganett, R. S. (1990). *Skills for living: Group counseling activities for young adolescents*. Champaign, IL: Research Press.

Mowrer, O. H. (1950). Identification: A link between learning theory and psychotherapy. In *Learning theory and personality dynamics* (pp. 573–616). New York: Ronald Press.

Moynihan, D. P. (1965). *The Negro family: The case for national action*. Washington, DC: Office of Policy Planning & Research, U.S. Department of Labor.

Mueller, C. W., & Pope, H. (1977). Marital instability: A study of its transmission between generations. *Journal of Marriage and the Family, 39*, 83–93.

Mueller, D. P., & Cooper, P. W. (1986). Children of single parent families: How they fare as young adults. *Family Relations, 35*, 169–176.

Mussen, P. H. (1969). Early sex role development. In D. A. Goslin (Ed.), *Handbook of socialization theory and research* (pp. 707–731). Chicago: Rand McNally.

Musser, J. M. (1982). The relationship of father parenting style and father absence to feminine heterosexual relationships and personality adjustment. *Dissertation Abstracts International, 43*, 0895B. (University Microfilms No. 8216827).

National Commission on Children (1991, November 21). *USA Today.*

Needle, R. H., Su, S., & Doherty, W. J. (1990). Divorce, remarriage, and adolescent drug involvement: A longitudinal study. *Journal of Marriage and the Family, 52*, 157–169.

Nelson, C. V., Thompson, J. C., Jr., Rice, C. M., & Cooley, V. E. (1991). *The effect of participation in activities outside the school and family structure on substance use by middle and secondary school students.* Presented at the meetings of the Midwest Educational Research Association, Chicago.

Nelson, E. A., & Vangen, P. M. (1971). The impact of father absence upon heterosexual behaviors and social development of preadolescent girls in a ghetto environment. *Proceedings of the Annual Convention of the American Psychological Association, 6*, 165–166.

Nelson, P. T. (1986). Newsletters: an effective delivery mode for providing educational information and emotional support to single parent families? *Family Relations, 35*, 183–188.

Neubauer, P. G. (1960). The one-parent child and his Oedipal development. *Psychoanalytic Study of the Child, 15*, 286–309.

Neugebauer, R. (1989). Divorce, custody, and visitation: The child's point of view. In C. A. Everett, (Ed.), *Children of divorce: Developmental and clinical issues* (pp. 153–168). New York: Haworth.

Nichols, W. C. (1985). Family therapy with children of divorce. *Journal of Psychotherapy and the Family, 1*, 55–68.

Norton, A. J., & Glick, P. C. (1976). Marital instability: Past, present and future. *Journal of Social Issues, 32*, 5–20.

Offord, D. R., Abrams, N., Allen, N., & Poushinsky, M. (1979). Broken homes, parental psychiatric illness, and female delinquency. *American Journal of Orthopsychiatry, 49*(2), 252–264.

O'Leary, K. D., & Emery, R. E. (1984). Marital discord and child behavior problems. In M. D. Levine & P. Satz (Eds.), *Developmental variation and dysfunction* (pp. 345–364). New York: Academic.

Orthner, D. K., Brown, T., & Ferguson, D. (1976). Single-parent fatherhood: An emerging family lifestyle. *Family Coordinator, 25*, 429–437.

Paddock-Ellard, K., & Thomas, S. (1981). Attitudes of young adolescents toward marriage, divorce, and children of divorce. *Journal of Early Adolescence, 1*, 303–310.

Pardeck, J. A., & Pardeck, J. T. (1985). Bibliotherapy using a Neo-Freudian approach for children of divorced parents. *School Counselor, 32*, 313–317.

Pardeck, J. T. (1989). Bibliotherapy and the blended family. *Family Therapy, 16*, 215–226.

Parish, T. S. (1980). The relationship between factors associated with father loss and individuals' level of moral judgment. *Adolescence, 15*(59), 535–541.

Parish, T. S., & Copeland, T. (1981). The impact of father absence on moral development in females. *Sex Roles, 7*(6), 635–636.

Parish, T. S., & Kappes, B. M. (1980). Impact of father loss on the family. *Social Behavior and Personality, 8,* 107–112.

Parke, R. (1981). *Fathers.* Cambridge, MA: Harvard University Press.

Parsons, T. (1955). Family structure and the socialization of the child. In T. Parsons & R. F. Bales (Eds.), *Family socialization, and interaction process* (pp. 35–131). Glencoe, IL: Free Press.

Pasley, K., & Ihinger-Tallman, M. (1982). Stress in second families. *Family Perspective, 16,* 181–196.

Pederson, F. A. (1976). Does research on children reared in father-absent families yield information on father influences? *Family Coordinator, 25,* 459–464.

Pederson, F. A., Rubenstein, J. L., & Yarrow, L. J. (1979). Infant development in father-absent families. *Journal of Genetic Psychology, 135*(1), 51–61.

Pedro-Carroll, J. L., & Cowen, E. L. (1985). The Children of Divorce Intervention Program: An investigation of the efficacy of a school-based prevention program. *Journal of Consulting and Clinical Psychology, 53,* 603–611.

Pedro-Carroll, J. L., Cowen, E. L., Hightower, A. D., & Guare, J. C. (1986). Preventive intervention with latency-aged children of divorce: A replication study. *American Journal of Community Psychology, 14,* 277–290.

Peterson, J. L., & Zill, N. (1986) Marital disruption, parent-child relationships, and behavior problems in children. *Journal of Marriage and the Family, 44,* 295–307.

Peterson, R. R. (1989). Women, work, and divorce. Albany: State University of New York Press.

Pfeifer, G., & Abrams, L. (1984). School-based discussion groups for children of divorce: A pilot program. *Group, 8,* 22–28.

Phares, V., & Compas, B. E. (1992). The role of fathers in child and adolescent psychopathology: Make room for daddy. Psychological Bulletin, Vol. III, pp. 387-412.

Pietropinto, A. (1985). Effect of unhappy marriages on children. *Medical Aspects of Human Sexuality, 19,* 173–181.

Plant, J. S. (1944). The psychiatrist views children of divorced parents. *Law and Contemporary Problems, 10,* 806–818.

Pleck, J. H. (1981). *The myth of masculinity.* Cambridge, MA: Massachusetts Institute of Technology Press.

Pleck, J. H. (1990). *Family-supportive employer policies: Are they relevant to men?* Paper presented for the American Psychological Association, Boston.

Pope, H., & Mueller, C. W. (1976). The intergenerational transmission of marital instability: Comparisons by race and sex. *Journal of Social Issues, 32,* 49–66.

Power, M. J., Ash, P. M., Shoenberg, E., & Sirey, E. C. (1974). Delinquency and the family. *British Journal of Social Work, 4*(1), 13–38.

Rankin, J. H. (1983). The family context of delinquency. *Social Problems, 30*(4), 466–479.

Raschke, H. J., & Raschke, V. J. (1979). Family conflict and children's self-concepts: A comparison of intact and single-parent families. *Journal of Marriage and the Family, 41,* 367–374.

Ricciuti, A. E., & Scarr, S. (1990). Interaction of early biological and family risk factors in predicting cognitive development. *Journal of Applied Developmental Psychology, 11,* 1–12.

Riley, G. (1991). *Divorce: An American tradition.* New York: Oxford University Press.

Rist, R. C. (1970). Student social class and teacher expectation: The self-fulfilling prophecy in ghetto education. *Harvard Educational Review, 40,* 411–450.

Robinson, P., & Andersen, A. E. (1985). Anorexia nervosa in American Blacks. *Journal of Psychiatric Research, 19*, 183–188.

Robson, B. E. (1983). And they lived happily ever after: Marriage concepts of older adolescents. *Canadian Journal of Psychiatry, 28*, 646–649.

Rosen, L. (1970). The broken home and male delinquency. In M. Wolfgang, L. Savitz, & N. B. Johnston, (Eds.), *The sociology of crime and delinquency* (pp. 489–495). New York: Wiley.

Rosen, L., & Neilson, K. (1982). Broken homes. In L. Savitz & N. Johnston (Eds.), *Contemporary criminology*. New York: Wiley.

Rosenfeld, J. M., & Rosenstein, E. (1973). Toward a conceptual framework for the study of parent-absent families. *Journal of Marriage and the Family, 35*, 131–135.

Rosenthal, D., Leigh, G. K., & Elardo, R. (1985/1986). Home environments of three- to six-year old children from father-absent and two-parent families. *Journal of Divorce, 9*(2), 41–48.

Rossiter, A. B. (1988). A model for group intervention with preschool children experiencing separation and divorce. *American Journal of Orthopsychiatry, 58*, 387–396.

Rozendal, F. G. (1983). Halos vs. stigmas: Long-term effects of parent's death or divorce on college students' concepts of the family. *Adolescence, 18*, 947–955.

Rutter, M. (1971). Parent-child separation: Psychological effects on the children. *Journal of Child Psychology and Psychiatry, 12*, 233–260.

Rutter, M. (1979). Protective factors in children's responses to stress and disadvantage. In M. W. Kent & J. E. Rolf (Eds.), *Primary prevention of psychopathology: Social competence in children* (Vol. 3). Hanover, NH: University Press of New England.

Rutter, M., & Madge, N. (1976). *Cycles of disadvantage: A review of research*. London: Heinemann.

Saayman, G. S., & Saayman, R. V. (1988–89). The adversarial legal process and divorce: Negative effects upon the psychological adjustment of children. *Journal of Divorce, 12*, 329–348.

Sales, B., Manber, R., & Rohman, L. (1992). Social science research and child-custody decision making. *Applied and Preventive Psychology, 1*, 23–40.

Salzman, S. A. (1987, April). *Meta-analysis of studies investigating the effects of father absence on children's cognitive performance*. Paper presented at the meeting of the American Education Research Association, Washington, DC.

Sampson, R. J. (1987). Urban black violence: The effect of male joblessness and family disruption. *American Journal of Sociology, 93*(2), 348–382.

Santrock, J. W. (1975). Father absence, perceived maternal behavior, and moral development in boys. *Child Development, 46*(3), 753–757.

Santrock, J. W., & Madison, T. D. (1985). Three research traditions in the study of adolescents in divorced families: Quasi-experimental, developmental; clinical; and family sociological. *Journal of Early Adolescence, 5*, 115–128.

Santrock, J. W., Sitterle, K. A., & Warshak, R. A. (1988). Parent-child relationships in stepfather families. In P. Bronstein & C. P. Cowan (Eds.), *Fatherhood today*. New York: Wiley.

Santrock, J. W., & Tracy, R. L. (1978). Effects of children's family structure status on the development of stereotypes by teachers. *Journal of Educational Psychology, 70*, 754–757.

Santrock, J. W., & Warshak, R. (1979). Father custody and social development in boys and girls. *Journal of Social Issues, 35*, 112–125.

Santrock, J. W., Warshak, R. A., & Elliott, G. L. (1981). Social development and parent-child interaction in father-custody and stepmother families. In M. E. Lamb (Ed.), *Nontraditional families* (pp. 289–314). Hillsdale, NJ: Erlbaum.

Sauer, L. E., & Fine, M. A. (1988). Parent-child relationships in stepparent families. *Journal of Family Psychology, 1*, 434–451.

Scarr, S. (1984). *Mother care, other care.* New York: Basic Books.

Scarr, S. (1985). Constructing psychology: Making facts and fables for our times. *American Psychologist, 40*, 499–512.

Scherman, A., & Lepak, L. (1986). Children's perceptions of the divorce process. *Elementary School Guidance and Counseling, 21*, 29–36.

Schmidt, F. L. (1992). What do data really mean? Research findings, meta-analysis, and cumulative knowledge in psychology. *American Psychologist, 47*, 1173–1181.

Schnayer, R., & Orr, R. R. (1989). A comparison of children living in single-mother and single-father families. In C. A. Everett (Ed.), *Children of divorce: Developmental and clinical issues* (pp. 171–184). New York: Haworth.

Serbin, L. A., Powlishta, K. K., & Gulko, J. (1993). The development of sex typing in middle childhood. *Monographs of the Society for Research in Child Development, 58*(2).

Shaw, D. S., & Emery, R. E. (1987). Parental conflict and other correlates of the adjustment of school-age children whose parents have separated. *Journal of Abnormal Child Psychology, 15*, 269–281.

Shaw, L. B. (1982). High school completion for young women: Effects of low income and living with a single parent. *Journal of Family Issues, 3*, 147–163.

Sheridan, J. T., Baker, S. B., & de-Lissovoy, V. (1984). Structured group counseling and explicit bibliotherapy as in-school strategies for preventing problems in youth of changing families. *School Counselor, 32*, 134–141.

Shinn, M. (1978). Father absence and children's cognitive development. *Psychological Bulletin, 85*(2), 295–324.

Skolnick, A. (1991). *Embattled paradise: The American family in an age of uncertainty.* New York: Basic Books.

Slater, E. J., & Haber, J. D. (1984). Adolescent adjustment following divorce as a function of family conflict. *Journal of Consulting and Clinical Psychology, 52*, 920–921.

Smith, D. (1979). Sex and deviance: An assessment of major sociological variables. *The Sociological Quarterly, 20*(2), 183–195.

Smith, R. M., & Walters, J. (1978). Delinquent and nondelinquent males perceptions of their fathers. *Adolescence, 13*, 21–28.

Somers, A. R. (1979). Marital status, health, and use of health services. *Journal of the American Medical Association, 241*, 1818–1822.

Sorosky, A. D. (1977). The psychological effects of divorce on adolescents. *Adolescence, 12*, pp. 123–136.

Southworth, S., & Schwarz, J. C. (1987). Post-divorce contact, relationship with father, and heterosexual trust in female college students. *American Journal of Orthopsychiatry, 57*(3), 371–382.

Sprenkle, D. H., & Storm, C. L. (1983). Divorce-therapy outcome research: A substantive and methodological review. *Journal of Marital and Family Therapy, 10*, 239–258.

Springer, C., & Wallerstein, J. S. (1983). Young adolescents' responses to their parents' divorces. In L. A. Kurdek (Ed.), *Children and divorce* (pp. 15–27). San Francisco: Jossey-Bass.

Steinberg, L. (1987). Single parents, stepparents, and the susceptibility of adolescents to anti-social peer pressure. *Child Development, 58,* 269–275.

Steinman, S. (1981). The experience of children in a joint-custody arrangement: A report of a study. *American Journal of Orthopsychiatry, 51,* 403–414.

Stern, M., Northman, J., & Van Slyck, M. R. (1984). Father absence and adolescent "problem behaviors": Alcohol consumption, drug use, and sexual activity. *Adolescence, 19,* 301–312.

Stevenson, M. R. (1988, April). *Single parenting and child-training expectations in Black women of Middletown.* Paper presented at Women in the Year 2000: Utopian and Dystopian Visions, Indianapolis.

Stevenson, M. R. (1990, November). *Heterosexual relationships of offspring in single-mother families.* Presented at the meeting of the Society for the Scientific Study of Sex, Minneapolis.

Stevenson, M. R. (1991). Perceptions of relationship with father and sex-typed characteristics of offspring. *Sex Roles, 24,* 239–244.

Stevenson, M. R., & Black, K. N. (1988). Paternal absence and sex-role development: A meta-analysis. *Child Development, 59,* 793–814.

Stirtzinger, R. (1986). Where is my daddy's house? Preschool age children of divorce and transitional phenomena. *Journal of Divorce, 10,* 139–151.

Stirtzinger, R., & Cholvat, L. (1990). Preschool age children of divorce: Transitional phenomenon and the mourning process. *Canadian Journal of Psychology, 35,* 506–513.

Stolberg, A. L., & Cullen, P. M. (1983). Preventive interventions for families of divorce: The Divorce Adjustment Project. *New Directions for Child Development, 19,* 71–81.

Stolberg, A. L., & Garrison, K. M. (1985). Evaluating a primary prevention program for children of divorce. *American Journal of Community Psychology, 13,* 111–124.

Stolberg, A. L., & Mahler, J. L. (1989). Protecting children from the consequences of divorce: An empirically derived approach. *Prevention in Human Services, 7,* 161–176.

Stoneman, Z., Brody, G. H., & Burke, M. (1989). Marital quality, depression and inconsistent parenting: Relationships with observed mother-child conflict. *American Journal of Orthopsychiatry, 59,* 105–117.

Stroebe, W. S., & Stroebe, W. (1983). Who suffers more? Sex differences in health risks of the widowed. *Psychological Bulletin. 93,* 279–301.

Stull, D. E., & Kaplan, N. M. (1987). The positive impact of divorce mediation on children's behavior. *Mediation Quarterly, 18,* 53–59.

Summers, M., Summers, C., & Ascione, F. (in press). A comparison of sibling interaction in intact and single-parent families. *Journal of Divorce and Remarriage.*

Surbey, M. K. (1990). Family composition, stress, and the timing of human menarche. In T. E. Ziegler & F. B. Bercovitch (Eds.), *Socioendocrinology of primate reproduction* (pp. 11–32), New York: Wiley-Liss.

Svanum, S., Bringle, R. G., & McLaughlin, J. E. (1982). Father absence and cognitive performance in a large sample of six- to eleven-year-old children. *Child Development, 53,* 136–143.

Taylor, M. C., & Hall, J. A. (1982). Psychological androgyny: Theories, methods, and conclusions. *Psychological Bulletin, 92,* 347–366.

Tennant, C., Bebbington, P. E., & Hurry, J. (1980). Parental death in childhood and risk of adult depressive disorders: A review. *Psychological Medicine, 10,* 289–299.

Tennyson, R. A. (1967). Family structure and delinquent behavior. In M. W. Klein & B. G. Myerhoff (Eds.), *Juvenile gangs in context*. Englewood Cliffs, NJ: Prentice-Hall.

Theodore, G. (1990). *The divorce game*. Salt Lake City: Theodore Games.

Thoennes, N., & Tjaden, P. G. (1990). The extent, nature, and validity of sexual abuse allegations in custody-visitation disputes. *Child Abuse and Neglect, 14*, 151–163.

Thomas, C. W., & Sieverdes, C. M. (1975). Juvenile court intake: An analysis of discretionary decision-making. *Criminology, 12*, 413–432.

Thornton, A. (1985). Changing attitudes toward separation and divorce: Causes and consequences. *American Journal of Sociology, 90*(4), 856–872.

Thornton, A., & Camburn, D. (1987). The influence of the family on premarital sexual attitudes and behavior. *Demography, 24*(3), 323–340.

Toby, J. (1957). The differential impact of family disorganization. *American Sociological Review, 22*(5), 505–512.

Trunnell, T. L. (1968). The absent father's children's emotional disturbances. *Archives of General Psychiatry, 19*, 180–188.

Tuckman, J., & Regan, R. (1966). Intactness of the home and behavioral problems in children. *Journal of Child Psychology and Psychiatry, 7*, 225–233.

Uddenberg, N. (1976). Mother-father & daughter-male relationships: A comparison. *Archives of Sexual Behavior, 5*(1), 69–79.

USA Today (1989, October, 1).

USA Today (1992, July 2), page 4D.

U.S. Bureau of Census. (1992). Current Population Reports, Series P-20, No. 458, *Household and Family Characteristics: 1991*, Washington, DC: U.S. Government Printing Office.

Van Bergen, A. (1979). Relationship of early father absence on sexual attitudes and self concept of adult women. *Dissertation Abstracts International, 39*, 5528B-5529B.

Vandamme, T. H. P., & Schwartz, S. (1985). Father-absence and scholastic performance in primary school children. *Current Psychological Research & Reviews, fall*, 204–213.

Verbrugge, L. M. (1979). Marital status and health. *Journal of Marriage and the Family, 41*, 267–285.

Villwock, D. N., Peckscamp, J. R., & Black, K. N. (1990, May). *A comparison of determinants of offsprings' feelings of closeness to parents*. Paper presented at the meeting of the Midwestern Psychological Association, Chicago.

Vuchinich, S., Hetherington, E. M., Vuchinich, R. A., & Clingempeel, W. G. (1991). Parent-child interaction and gender differences in early adolescents' adaptation to stepfamilies. *Developmental Psychology, 27*, 618–626.

Walker, K. N., Rogers, J., & Messinger, L. (1977). Remarriage after divorce: A review. *Social Casework, 58*, 276–285.

Wallerstein, J. S. (1985a). Women after divorce: Preliminary report from a ten-year follow-up. *American Journal of Orthopsychiatry, 56*, 65–77.

Wallerstein, J. S. (1985b). Children of divorce: Preliminary report of a ten-year follow-up of older children and adolescents. *Journal of the American Academy of Child Psychiatry, 24*, 545–553.

Wallerstein, J. S. (1987). Children of divorce: Report of a ten-year follow-up of early latency-age children. *American Journal of Orthopsychiatry, 57*(2), 199–211.

Wallerstein, J. S. (1989, January 22). Children after divorce: Wounds that don't heal. *New York Times Magazine.*

Wallerstein, J. S. (1991). The long-term effects of divorce on children: A review. *Journal of the American Academy of Child and Adolescent Psychiatry, 30,* 349–360.

Wallerstein, J. S., & Blakeslee, S. (1989). *Second chances: Men, women, and children a decade after divorce.* New York: Ticknor & Fields.

Wallerstein, J. S., & Corbin, S. B. (1986). Father-child relationships after divorce: Child support and educational opportunity. *Family Law Quarterly, 20,* 109–128.

Wallerstein, J. S., & Kelly, J. B. (1974). The effects of parental divorce: The adolescent experience. In E. J. Anthony & C. Koupernik (Eds.), *The child in his family: Children at psychiatric risk* (pp. 479–506). New York: Wiley.

Wallerstein, J. S., & Kelly, J. B. (1980). *Surviving the breakup: How children actually cope with divorce.* New York: Basic Books.

Warren, N. J., & Amara, I. A. (1985). Educational groups for single parents: The Parenting After Divorce programs. *Journal of Divorce, 8,* 79–96.

Warshak, R. A. (1986). Father-custody and child development: A review and analysis of psychological research. *Behavioral Sciences & the Law, 4,* 185–202.

Warshak, R. A. (1987). Father-custody families: Therapeutic goals and strategies. In M. Lindblad-Goldberg (Ed.), *Clinical issues in single-parent households* (pp. 101–124). Rockville, MD: Aspen Publications.

Warshak, R. A., & Santrock, J. W. (1983a). The impact of divorce in father-custody and mother-custody homes: The child's perspective. In L. A. Kurdek (Ed.), *Children and divorce: New directions for child development* (pp. 29–46). San Francisco: Jossey-Bass.

Warshak, R. A., & Santrock, J. W. (1983b). Children of divorce: Impact of custody disposition on social development. In E. J. Callahan & K. A. McCluskey, (Eds.), *Life-span developmental psychology: Normative life events* (pp. 241–263). New York: Academic Press.

Webster-Stratton, C., & Hammond, M. (1990). Predictors of treatment outcome in parent training for families with conduct problem children. *Behavior Therapy, 21,* 319–337.

Weiss, R. S. (1979). Growing up a little faster: The experience of growing up in a single-parent household. *Journal of Social Issues, 35,* 97–111.

Weitzman, L. J. (1985). *The divorce revolution: The unexpected social and economic consequences for women and children in America.* New York: Free Press.

Wentzel, K. R. (1991). Relations between social competence and academic achievement in early adolescence. *Child Development, 62,* 1066–1078.

Westman, J. C. (1972). Effects of divorce on a child's personality development. *Medical Aspects of Human Sexuality, 6,* 38–55.

White, L. K., Brinkerhoss, D. B., & Booth, A. (1985). The effect of marital disruption on child's attachment to parents. *Journal of Family Issues, 6,* 5–22.

Whitehead, B. D. (1993, July). Divorce and kids: The evidence is in. *Reader's Digest,* 118–123.

Whitley, B. E. (1983). Sex role orientation and self-esteem: A critical meta-analytic review. *Journal of Personality and Social Psychology, 44,* 765–778.

Whitley, B. E. (1985). Sex-role orientation and psychological well-being: Two meta-analyses. *Sex Roles, 12,* 207–225.

Wijnberg, M. H., & Holmes, T. (1992). Adaptation to divorce: The impact of role orientation on family-life-cycle perspectives. *Families in Society, 73,* 159–167.

Wilkinson, K. (1980). The broken home and delinquent behavior: An alternative interpretation of contradictory findings. In T. Hirschi & M. Gottfredson (Eds.), *Understanding crime: Current theory and research* (pp. 21–42). Beverly Hills: Sage.

Williams, B. M., Wright, D., & Rosenthal, D. (1983). A model for intervention with latency-aged children of divorce. *Family Therapy, 10,* 111–124.

Winch, R. F. (1949). Relationship between loss of parent and progress in courtship. *Journal of Social Psychology, 29,* 51–56.

Wineberg, H. (1992). Childbearing and dissolution of the second marriage. *Journal of Marriage and the Family, 54,* 879–887.

Woodman, J. I., & Lewis, G. J. (1990). The coparental relationship of divorced spouses: Its effect on children's school adjustment. *Journal of Divorce and Remarriage, 14,* 81–95.

Woody, J. D., Colley, P. E., Schlegelmilch, J., Maginn, P., & Balsanek, J. (1984). Child adjustment to parental stress following divorce. *Social Casework, 65,* 405–412.

Worobey, J. L., Angel, R. J., & Worobey, J. (1988). Family structure and young children's use of medical care. *Topics in Early Childhood Special Education, 8,* 30–40.

Young, E. R., & Parish, T. S. (1977). Impact of father absence during childhood on the psychological adjustment of college females. *Sex Roles, 3,* 217–227.

Zaslow, M. J. (1988). Sex differences in children's response to parental divorce: I. Research methodology and postdivorce family forms. *American Journal of Orthopsychiatry, 58,* 355–378.

Zaslow, M. J. (1989). Sex differences in children's response to parental divorce: II. Samples, variables, ages, and sources. *American Journal of Orthopsychiatry, 59,* 118–141.

Zembar, M. J., Behrendt, T., & Etz, K. (1991, April). *Sibling relationships in pre-and post-divorce families.* Paper presented at the meetings of the Society for Research in Child Development, Seattle.

Zients, A. B. (1986). Identification and its vicissitudes as observed in adolescence: Object loss and identification. *International Journal of Psycho-Analysis, 67,* 77–85.

Zill, N. (1978, February) *Divorce, marital happiness, and the mental health of children: Findings from the FCD national survey of children.* Paper presented at the NIMH Workshop on Divorce and Children, Bethesda, MD.

INDEX